Cowboys
Are Not Supposed to
CRY

And the Best Thing You Can Do with Death Is to Ride off from It?

A MEMOIR

Mark W. Schutter

ISBN 978-1-63903-102-3 (paperback)
ISBN 978-1-63903-103-0 (digital)

Christian Faith Publishing, Inc.
832 Park Avenue
Meadville, PA 16335
www.christianfaithpublishing.com

Printed in the United States of America

DEDICATION

This book is dedicated to the following:

1. *Carri darlin'*, my beautiful wife and warrior queen, you saved me so many years ago and have stood by my side ever since. Your strength and devotion have helped heal my heart and mind. You are a gift and have always shown me the true meaning of love, courage, loyalty, and grace.
2. *Charis (Muppin)*, my beautiful daughter, you are the truest embodiment of a warrior princess. You have blessed my life beyond compare. You are a miracle and everything a father could want in a daughter—fearless, brave, caring, funny, adventurous, and loving.

Blessed are those who mourn, for they shall be comforted.

—Matthew 5:4 NASB

CONTENTS

FOREWORD

As a counseling psychologist in private practice for over thirty years, I get the chance to work with some truly amazing people. I get the privilege of walking with others through the most difficult times of their life. It is a journey I feel honored to make. Few have felt more rewarding or moving than my knowing and working with Mark. His story is painful, honest, deep, and thought-provoking. As I walked together with him on his journey of healing, there were many times I was moved to tears (I am not a big crier), and on a few occasions, I had to resist weeping. More than once, I sat after one of our meetings and pondered how deeply the meeting impacted me. It made me appreciate life, want to be better, and want to love more deeply.

Reading Mark's story will most likely do the same for you. This book is for people who have had real pain, people who have loved and lost and are struggling to move on, men and women who have lost a spouse like Mark or a child or a career or a war or some other trauma that marks one's life. I believe the reader will be enthralled in how Mark walks through his pain and, in the process, be helped and inspired.

This book is especially for men. We men tend to bury our pain rather than process it through. Thus, we stay stuck and limited in how we live. Mark dives deeply into his pain and, in turn, helps us to go there too. It is not a self-help book, but it will definitely be a help to self. I believe by reading this, men can learn how to walk through their pain, even though their pain may be different. Reading Mark's story will help men deal with grief and pain and, in the end, want to live life well. Life doesn't stop with pain. Pain can be a bridge to a new life. Mark's story will inspire men to walk over that bridge, to appreciate life, to love deeper, and in the end be better men…maybe even a cowboy.

Jeffrey D. Wagaman, PhD
Counseling Psychologist
Cascade Counseling, President

ACKNOWLEDGMENTS

I want to acknowledge the following for their part in my story,

Almighty God, Jesus, and Holy Spirit—thank you. You are my strength, hope, and salvation in this life and the life to come.

Family and friends—there are too many to name individually, and yet they have all played a major part in my story, in this story. Thank you for your love, support, kindness, and truth.

The team at Christian Faith Publishing—thank you to every individual who had a hand in making this book come to be a reality, for believing in my story and me.

You, the reader—I pray my story, my struggles and healing, may strengthen you and serve as a reminder that you are not alone, for if we do not have hope, we have nothing.

Luka—there are so many words I wanted to say and never took the chance. However, it does not need saying; I will see you again someday.

INTRODUCTION

*To know even one life has breathed easier because
you have lived—that is to have succeeded.*
—Ralph Waldo Emerson

As I look back over my life, the questions haunt me. Have I succeeded? How do you define a successful life? Can you ever truly return to a moment once it has passed? Or return to a time that has vanished into a room behind a door locked for all eternity? Is there hope in a return to an ending that is now somehow a beginning?

The flash of smoke slips through your fingers, the moments are quickly gone, and we are clutching nothing. We are alone as time slips from our hands. A once-and-forever slice of time that is a piece of you disappears into the past. We are never the same, hearts forever changed living now under a different-colored sky. So many dreams now vanished into the seemingly endless dark black of night, and faint slivers of hope are all we have left.

This is my story, my reality, my life, and this book explores but a few of the many questions I have asked. The twinges of memory flit across my mind as a butterfly haunts a flower. Yes, you could say my story has left me bitter...hell, truthfully even to this very day, I sometimes do not know what I am. And yes, you might rightly say I am sometimes jaded.

My experiences are sure to be vastly different from others, and some commonality may resonate. Yet this is my story and my voice screaming unanswered questions into the overwhelming silence. I still stare into the nighttime sky, sometimes as dark as death where stars twinkle on unconcerned, and the cold vastness reveals little measure of comfort to assuage my pain and longing that I have chosen to still carry.

I do know that I am strong, and this will not defeat me. I am working hard on the next chapter of my life to make it mean something. I will bang a drum for those we have lost and never assume to understand someone else's experience and pain for I would never expect the two to be the same. I believe in the *ripple effect*—touch one life, and you may touch the world.

Life, while we are alive, goes on whether we want it to or not in that we do not get a choice.

Events happen throughout our lives; hard times come with often no end in sight. Loved ones die, and there is often no response from beyond the veil, only silence. There is a vast undiscovered that beckons silently to us all with oftentimes no confirmation of what may come. Do we silently maintain faith with an expectation of the glorious promises of what may come?

Death once took all I had and all I thought I would ever be, my future and so much yet undiscovered. I walked through my own the valley of shadow, the questions from my broken heart often met only stony silence, my many sins repeated wrapped in survivor's guilt and shame that still hounds my steps and haunts the doors of my heart. My heart and soul is often a lonely place, and I find I must rise again daily from the ash heap.

When we suffer loss, when it finds us in one form or another, we must first reconcile our past. Second, we must embrace the present, our circumstances, and play the cards life has dealt us. Thirdly, we must redeem our future, a vision with new dreams for a new life where there is no finish line. Forever changed, we must move forward. A different person with a different trajectory, we carry the past with us every step of the way. Grief and loss change us; how could they not?

As time passes, there begins again a new flame that burns bright, an inferno that scorches my already scarred heart. From the fires, I have hidden deep forgotten memories in the dark. It grows again. The light chases the ghosts, stoking new passions to fly and soar over every self-imposed wall. My life has come full circle amid visions of hope that rise despite the memories of death, while a hole remains because healing is often messy, difficult, and not perfect, and that is okay.

.

AUTHORS NOTE

This story is based on real true-life events; however as memories often fade and tend to change over time, specific details may or may not be entirely accurate, and I may have taken certain liberties as creative non-fiction. I have endeavored to recall the events as best that I can and be assured the stories of my relationship with Luka, her death, the impacts on me, my healing, and underlying message is true as I lived it. When I began writing this book, I also finally took seriously my own unresolved grief. The healing I have experienced in the past few years is available to all if only we would choose it. God bless and live your dreams!

Mark W. Schutter
February 2021

GRIEF

By Charis Emily

they all say grief is grey.

but it's not.

it's blazing white fury that saturates your vision and blinds you, consuming your mind in a thunderous, raging tempest. it's the black coolness of your room at 2am, when you're sobbing into your pillow, and there's only the walls to bear witness to your illicit agony. it's fiery scarlet fits of unforeseen, heart-wrenching torment, as you scream out desperate questions, to which there are no answers. it's the beguiling, soothing blue of a river flowing past, smoothing down the angst-ridden ruffles of your heart, letting peace fill the quiet, melancholy air around you. it's the bright colors—the pinks and violets and metallics—swirling around inside of you like a whirlpool of emotions, uncontrollable. it's the nostalgic, honey-gold glow of the wonderful memories that brought you so much light and joy; still tainting the air around you, even long after those memories have set in the western sky. it's the deep purple of your inner-most ache, resounding through the walls of your chest, like the long, lonely echoes of a cave, settling into your bones forevermore. it's the ugliest, muddled brown of every paint oozing and blending together; as it pools down, gradually picking up speed until it's cascading like a landslide on top of you; and you're digging your fingers into your scalp as you feel your life falling apart in an array of tumultuous fear, and it seizes your throat with panic, so that you cannot breathe.

and sometimes, it is the grey of a drizzly, overcast day. as you feel the numb and hopeless exhaustion of sorrow, dripping slowly into your heart, filling you to the brim, tainting your whole body, your whole vision, your whole world.

grief comes in a splendid rainbow of colors, ebbing and flowing like a tide as you attempt to ride the waves of this unexplainable emotion, praying to God, that you don't sink.

Part 1

RECONCILING
THE PAST

CHAPTER 1

Out of the Sun

If I find in myself a desire which no experience
in this world can satisfy, the most probable expla-
nation is that I was made for another world.
—C. S. Lewis, *Mere Christianity*

"Hello" was all she said. A simple little word started it all. As I walk the hallways of my mind after almost thirty years, there is a memory of a girl with long brown hair and piercing blue eyes. She is wearing a colorful summer dress and espadrilles sandals as the lyrics to the Al Stewart song "Year of the Cat" ring in my head. I can still picture in my mind the vivid sunlit watercolor hues running in the rain the moment she walked into my life.

Luka—that is what I always called her from the beginning. Her given name was Ruth Ann; Luka was a nickname, and it fit her perfectly. She grew up as a missionary kid, mostly in the Philippines. It was the fall of 1984, a typical southwestern Idaho early autumn. The mornings were cool; the temperature steadily climbing as the day warmed until it began its plummet as evening's chill set in. The trees that lined the Boise River had begun their annual dance of color as the leaves began their own yearly journey toward death.

I was a young man tittering on the edge of adulthood who wore jeans, cowboy boots, and flannel shirts. The only certainty in my life was that I knew I did not know who I was. I had no idea who I was becoming or what direction to go in.

I had grown up mostly country, I guess, played some sports through middle and high school; just a regular kid. Known by the cool crowd but not enough to hang with them and not fitting in under the glare of the city lights, I yearned for wide-open spaces. I would say I was not a true "jock" and I was not a "freak" either, having never had smoked nor drunk during high school. I often found myself caught between worlds I did not always understand. I was just there trying to stand in the middle of the swift currents of late adolescence and trying to find my way.

I was now entering my second year of college after sitting out a semester and working. That fall, it was her clear blue eyes, brown hair, and tanned skin that caught my eye. The summer sun had turned her skin the color of light mocha all the way down to the tops of her feet. After that initial meeting in a watercolor painting class, a friendship quickly blossomed. We would sit under a tree outside the liberal arts building on the campus of Boise State University, basking in the soft fall breezes under blue skies. As we sat in the cool green grass, she would kick off her shoes, and the tan lines across the top of her feet caused by the espadrille sandals she wore was in stark contrast to the white alabaster skin of her toes. Just above the tan line on both of her feet was a jagged pink scar. The scar ran across the top of both feet from one side to the other in sharp contrast from the straight edge of the tan lines. I wondered at that line for many days, until I finally I got up the nerve to ask.

Luka told me about the incisions where they had inserted dye into her bloodstream to test for the spread of the Hodgkin's disease when she was younger, a forever reminder of a battle she must always be ready to fight in regards to her health. We talked for hours, and Luka told me of her past battle with disease and the things she suffered. This simple inquisitive question about a physical mark opened the doors to conversations of life, death, and faith.

I was quiet and insecure, and a path she showed to me opened the world before my eyes. It seems such a little thing, but it meant so much that what I remember is her encouraging me to be who I was created to be. I am sure others had told me this also, but as a young man, when a beautiful brown-haired young woman with soulful blue eyes looks intently at you, you take notice and pay attention to what she says.

Music and Memories

Early in our relationship, one night, she played the 1983 Michael W. Smith song "Friends" for me. Holding a cassette tape in her hand, she simply said, "I have a song I want to play for you."

"Okay," I responded and went and grabbed my little cassette tape recorder. We sat in silence as the song played, and she watched me intently. I listened closely to the lyrics and the melody coming through the little speakers. As the song ended, she delicately pushed the stop button on the player, and the silence engulfed us. After several seconds, she asked somewhat shyly, "So what do think?"

That simple question led to a long discussion on God, life, theology, faith, and our purpose here on earth. It was the beginning of my deeper dive into my faith and search for truth. Her upbringing as a missionary's kid and attending a Christian-run school in the Philippines gave her a much greater knowledge of the Bible than I had at that time. She introduced me to Christian music and bands like Petra, Whiteheart as well as Amy Grant, Bryan Duncan, Sandi Patti, Second Chapter of Acts, and so many more.

I had grown up on country music and a little bit of rock and roll, an odd combination of Marie and Donny Osmond, I guess. In high school, I drifted to some harder rock music, mostly based on peer pressure of friends, and some Top 40 music that blared out of the car windows of fellow students in the high school parking lots. When Luka and I met, I was listening to Tanya Tucker's "Delta Dawn," Alabama's "If You're Gonna Play in Texas," and George Strait's "Amarillo by Morning" among others.

She shared with me her love of the music of Al Jarreau's "Roof Garden" and Sade's "Smooth Operator," a different kind of music I never experienced. It was a world I had never paid any attention to before. The soulful sounds of jazz created a storm over me as powerful as the bright lights of a big city, opening up a completely new world. Music became a backdrop to our relationship, and the REO Speedwagon song "Can't Fight This Feeling" became our song. It summed up our relationship and the feelings that grew from a friendship.

We traveled through those first few years together as we looked toward a future that was wide open. Luka's strong, steadfast belief in a God that provided for all his children intrigued and captivated me. We went on walks across the campus from the sorority house where she lived, marveling in creation and just being together. One special night in December, we passed by the large evergreen tree in the center of the commons all decked out in Christmas lights for the upcoming holiday. It was a cold cloudless night with a million stars twinkling in the sky. We encountered an old black lab wandering the campus, and he followed us for a while before making his way off in another direction disappearing into the dark.

I remember the simple things from the beginning of our lives together. We lived in those moments that held special meaning to us but seemed so ordinary in their significance. We played tennis late at night on the lighted campus courts. Carrying our shoes, we danced barefoot in the rain along city sidewalks in the warm summer rain showers, not caring what others thought. This was our life, and her passion for life became a force that let me live and feel fully alive.

We took long drives into the surrounding high mountain desert, seeing coyotes, rabbits, and hawks soaring overhead, often stopping at a Chinese restaurant where the owner came to know us by name. We would order take out, the same thing every time. Our stomachs were growling from the warm aroma of food wafting from the bag containing sweet and sour chicken, fried rice, and egg rolls which surrounded us in the air as we drove. We would eat together, scraping the food from the little cardboard boxes with plastic forks while watching the sunset and the emergence of the stars. We talked about our dreams of the future. The high desert of southern Idaho became our escape from the pressures and tasks of life and the obligations of two young college students with an unknown future ahead of them.

I remember her sparkling earrings and skin so brown, the high mountain desert, and a billion stars twinkling overhead. The Eagles' song "Peaceful Easy Feeling" is an anthem that still reminds me of her, a future all wrapped up in a moment and in dreams to grow old together and the adventures we would share, even, children if God willed it. There was so much to live for, so much to look forward to, while a haunting voice whispered there will come a time when I will never see her again.

And it was much sooner than I ever expected. I did not know how true those words were at the time. The memories remain, but the warmth of her touch has long since faded.

It Begins

Luka had joined a sorority the semester after we met and we spent many nights together and it was there in the dark of the house, alone, where we first pledged our love for one another. She opened my eyes to so much more, and I knew this girl was all I wanted.

She became my best friend, my mentor, my teacher, and my lover in the end. Never contemplating my past before the end, this young girl opened so many doors. Looking back, I see now there are lives that come together, intersecting at the perfect time. She was a gift, and her joy helped me traverse my way in a world so cold. It seems now that from that first moment our eyes met, our time together was preparing me for the day she had to leave me. I believe she knew that this was a temporary thing, and she had to go and could not stay, for everything she did, in big ways and small ways, was quickly preparing me for a future I never imagined.

She walked into my life at the beginning of a college freshman watercolor painting class. I had taken painting classes through high school, and I was looking forward to learning all that I could and growing my art skills, especially in this area. Little did I know that what God had planned for me was so much more than a simple art class. This one decision to pursue an art degree with a teaching credential would affect the rest of my life in profound and painful ways. It was the first few days of that watercolor class when our eyes met for the first time.

I sat alone at the rectangular table set up for two students in a 100-college level watercolor painting class, waiting nervously for class to begin. Thoughts of doubt swirled in my head. Was I any good as an artist? How good were the other students, and would I even measure up? Could I measure up? Did I really know what I was doing? Did I have any real talent? These thoughts coursed through my head, and my heart raced, my stomach in knots of apprehension as I sat there stoically, trying hard to look relaxed but not making eye contact with other students as they filed into the room.

I heard the laughter, turned toward the sound, and looking up, it was the eyes that captured my attention first. Those blue eyes held me transfixed, eyes that sparkled reflections of the deepest blue. She entered the room with another female student who, to this day, I have no recollection other than she was there. It was the fall of 1984, and life—my life—would never be the same.

I stole looks at the most vivid blue eyes I had ever seen as they occasionally locked onto mine. The beauty of those blue eyes and the extraordinarily beautiful brown-haired young woman that accompanied them stunned me. It was days before we actually spoke more than a hesitant hello and distracted glances, the first words have long since vanished into memory.

I recall that sometime during those first few weeks of class on one otherwise seemingly normal day, my world changed when the utterly remarkable happened. She entered the classroom where I was already setting up my painting supplies and was suddenly walking straight toward me. She placed her own art supplies on the table in the empty place next to me and sat in the chair next to mine. Her voice so sweet and her laughter lit up the room as the other students seemed to fade before my eyes. As our eyes locked for a split second, eternity knocked on the door of my heart.

In later conversations, she told me that her girlfriend she normally sat next to was absent that day. She did not know why she walked over to the table I was sitting at, only that it seemed to be destined, as if she had no choice in the matter. It was what she was supposed to do, and she could only obey.

The conversation that day was minimal, nothing more than formality and casual politeness. My hands shook, and my stomach was in knots throughout. That one moment spilled into days and weeks, lost in painting side by side and in the conversation as a friendship began to blossom as, later, summer turned into autumn. We shared many talks between classes under a tree outside the liberal arts building. It was here that I learned about her life growing up as a missionary's kid in the Philippines, her trouble with a previous boyfriend, how she adored her grandfather, her strained relationship with her grandmother, and the recent death of her beloved cat.

She relayed that often, when returning to the States, she would find herself in a state of adjustment, feeling very out of place and in culture shock. She commented to me on several occasions when communicating her experiences that she would often wish to return to the Philippines shortly after arriving back in the States.

Even though she was born in America, she never seemed to feel truly comfortable here. She found herself homesick for the country in which she had lived for most of her formative years. The people and the culture were what she knew best, many times stating that in her young mind, the Philippines, the world, the life she knew and had created for herself there was home.

Although she also believed that, this world was not her home either. She believed and helped me to believe that there was a far better place, a place that existed out past the sun, where it rained colors and memories never faded, where the last became first and the pain became joy and you traveled via the slipstream, a place where we can let go of the pain, the loss, and the death of this world.

CHAPTER 2

A Far Better Place

If I could have seen the end from the begin-
ning I still would not have changed a thing.
                                        —Mark Wayne

"You know this is serious, right?"

My tone was hushed as if afraid my voice would usher in the
finality of the statement as it echoed in the silence of the room. I sat
on the edge of the hospital bed, moving slowly so as not to jostle the
mattress. The slightest noise bounced off the walls like a rubber ball
in a pinball machine, the echoes of each little sound lingering long
after.

The sound of the medical machinery hummed in the darkness
of the room, a constant deafening reminder that the precious seconds
were ticking by. Each second brought us both closer to the abyss. We
were approaching the void hand in hand, and I knew that eventually,
invisible forces would tear us apart.

For several moments after I spoke, Luka lay unmoving. I waited,
watching silently as her eyes slowly focused, and she looked directly
at me. We gazed at each other as her head slowly nodded yes to my
question. I gently squeezed her hand and forced a smile, which she

returned, an almost imperceptible movement of her lips that easily could have went unnoticed if I had not known her so well. Taking a deep slow breath, she closed her eyes, her head resting on the pillow. Her now shorter dark-brown hair splayed out in sharp contrast to the white of the hospital pillow cover. I continued to sit silently as I watched her drift back to sleep. After several moments, I glanced at the clock sitting on a shelf on the wall above the head of the bed. The red LED numbers read 2:32 a.m.; it was now Good Friday, April 9, 1993.

Letting go of her hand, I made my way quietly to the dark-brown recliner that was next to the utilitarian hospital bed where she lay. For the next few hours, I sat alone watching her sleep, knowing that time was short, my heart silently reeling. Time ticked slowly away, marching toward dawn unconcerned as another arcing of life and death played out. An unseen strength carried me forward into the early morning hours of a new day.

The events of the last twenty-four hours that had brought us both to this point danced on the fringes of my mind as a dream. I pondered the immensity of the moment and the irreducible serious-ness that was before us, clinging to some small hope, and that was the only speck of truth I allowed myself to believe in, for everything else was too heavy to bear.

Thursday, the day before, was a plethora of tests until finally admitting Luka into the hospital as a patient as her condition con-tinued to worsen. Early Thursday evening, I excused myself from the small throng of family and friends in Luka's hospital room and approached her oncologist in the hallway where he stood talking on a wall phone after completing his evening check-in with her.

Luka had been calling him by his first name shortly after meet-ing him as she was not one to stand on formality. She had a way about her, an easygoing style and charm that disarmed people with a smile and generosity that was unmistakably real and genuine.

Seeing me approach, the doctor nodded and held up a hand, motioning for me to wait for him to finish. I stood, trying to quell my anxiety, not fully aware of where I was as each breath caught in my lungs, heavy and suffocating. Hanging up the wall phone, he turned toward me, and I stepped forward, closing the distance between us. I do not remember the words he first spoke, but the look on his face left no doubt as to the situation and Luka's condition.

I felt a million miles away from my body, and I heard myself say with great effort, "I only want her to not be in pain."

He looked at me with a look of both sadness and resignation, his voice low and measured. "That is what I am focused on."

I nodded in agreement, and he turned and walked away. I watched him stride down the hall, his white lab coat flying out at his sides. Standing for a moment alone, I collected myself amid the noise of the hospital corridor. Forcing myself to turn, I slowly walked back into the hospital room. I plastered a smile on my face and buried the fear so far down where I believed it could never be unearthed. Thus began the long lonely vigil of Luka's last night on earth, our final moment of connection and, ultimately, our separate journeys.

Alone into the Alone

They say that death is not the end, just another beginning beyond our sight. Heaven is what exists over the horizon. We just cannot see it, but it is there where true glory exists. In those moments of fear and darkness, it seems like a fanciful tale, full of rage and fury, platitudes and soggy sandwiches. We can never be truly sure until we cross that boundary for ourselves and journey into the undiscovered.

Only death truncates the pain of this life. The unrelenting ache in her body continued to spread like water, seeking a path of least resistance over arid ground. It continued to grow, never ending, never ceasing, and I could only stand helplessly by and watch as she endured to the end, sometimes with silence, sometimes with whimpers and quiet tears, and other times with screams of anguish and torment, this unseen foe growing inside that often ripped apart her soul and mine as well.

It had only been two short years since the first diagnosis, two years that now seemed a lifetime ago when this nightmare had begun. In January 1990, we moved to Bellingham, Washington, from Boise so I could take a promotional opportunity at work. We settled in, making friends and a new life for ourselves in this little city by the bay at the top of Puget Sound just miles from the Canadian border. After a short time, Luka began working at the children's museum in downtown Bellingham as the events coordinator. That fall, she felt a lump in her breast, and she went to the doctor who ordered a biopsy.

We got the results within a week, and the bad news was it was cancer, breast cancer, a word I was very unfamiliar with except at a great distance. The doctor immediately recommended an ultra-radical mastectomy to remove her right breast, all the lymph nodes up and under her armpit and the surrounding tissue.

It was trying times, just the two of us with no family close. I was struggling in the new job, trying to fit in but also taking time off to take care of my wife. Following the surgery, Luka came home to recover. She was sore and hurting, the physical pain immense from the surgery. The cats and the dog were very happy to see her in our little one-bedroom rental house.

However, after a few days, my boss, who I stressed over getting on his bad side due to the stories I had heard from others, asked me when I was coming back to work. Against my better judgment, I left my wife alone at home and went back to work. After a full day at work, I came home that evening. Luka was extremely upset, almost hysterical, as she cried in my arms. Between sobs she said she had never felt so alone or so unlovable in all her life.

While showering, she had cried and cried because of the ugliness and disfigurement she felt about her body. She felt horrid, unattractive, despondent, and hopeless. I held my wife in a strong embrace, wishing I could make her pain go away. The guilt over my inability to protect her washed over me.

The surgeon had inserted a port-a-cath device under her skin prior to Luka leaving the hospital. It entered her body just above her one remaining breast. A long plastic tube extended into a central vein into which they injected the chemotherapy drugs.

The long clear plastic tube extended outside of her body. We wound this tube into small circles and placed it inside her empty bra cup during nonuse. My responsibility was to remove the cap and flush the tube every morning and night with a saline solution mixture in between the chemotherapy visits. Using a hypodermic needle, I drew solution from a container, then inserted the needle into the end of the catheter tube and slowly pushed the stopper to flush the tube clean. Luka complained that she could taste metal in her mouth, a horrible feeling making her want to gag.

This became our daily routine for weeks of chemotherapy treatments. Luka had resumed working part time. Our lives took on a normal routine, and the chemotherapy treatments and side effects were part of that. Following a few rounds of chemo and shortly after Christmas, Luka's left arm began to swell. X-rays revealed a large blood clot in her arm. They immediately admitted her to the hospital due to fears of the clot breaking free. They put her on an IV drip solution to dissolve the clot, putting a halt to further chemotherapy treatments for the time being.

Luka was in the hospital for a little over a week. It was a lonely time for her and for me. Each day seemed eerily the same. I would get up early to take care of the animals, head to the hospital, spend time with her before heading to work. Following work, I would return to the hospital, usually picking up some food along the way before heading back home to take care of the animals and get a few hours of sleep and repeat the whole scenario over again. Being tied to the IV drip bag all the time and stuck in the hospital weighed heavily on both of us.

I found myself becoming very self-reliant and comfortable, if you could call it that, with the routine at the hospital. I knew my way around and used a back, less busy entrance to enter and exit which got me to her room quicker and easier. This door avoided the more crowded waiting room, patient entrance, and normal entries. Hospital staff never once questioned or tried to stop me.

I walked as if I belonged there; I was a man on a mission. I can only assume those who saw me presumed I knew where I was going. Once in the elevator, another person looked at me and asked me, "Are you a doctor?"

"No," I replied, and as the elevator door opened, I quickly exited and walked away smiling.

The blood clot dissolved after just over a week, and following discharge from the hospital, they scheduled another round of chemotherapy. She endured the procedure, and the dreaded two days of nausea and hell followed as I watched helpless. My life as a husband to a wife fighting breast cancer continued, and every day was a reminder.

Shortly thereafter, late one evening in January, we sat in the children's museum on the children's oversized toys talking about our future, the next steps, and where this was leading us. She was tired of the treatments. She was tired of the whole thing. And she told me she felt in her heart of hearts that the chemotherapy was not doing any good, and she wanted to stop. She reasoned, and the oncologist had told us that the treatments were only a preventative measure. All the surrounding tissue and lymph nodes were clean following the mastectomy. I was scared, but I trusted my wife. She had never lied to me before, and I agreed with her that we would stop the chemotherapy. The oncology doctor seemed surprised, but he did not try to talk us out of it. We focused on his comment that he was optimistic that they had gotten the entire tumor.

We scheduled an appointment with the surgeon to have the port-a-cath tube removed. Again we were reassured this was an easy outpatient visit to the doctor's office. As Luka sat on the paper-covered examining room table with only her bra on, the doctor talked to her while I stood quietly by her side listening.

The thin plastic tubing extended a good foot and a half outside of her body and the skin tissue around had healed and grown over the edge of the tube, forming scar tissue around the insertion site. I watched as the doctor slowly wrapped the tube around his hand, which he held down at his side.

Oh my god, I thought. It all started happening in slow motion, and I could do nothing to stop the awful movie I was watching.

He continued to talk to Luka, distracting her from what he was doing. I watched as he slowly completed wrapping the tube around his hand. My eyes went to her face just before he jerked his hand downward, the skin around the tube ripping as Luka let out a little shriek of pain. I saw the surprise in her eyes. The rest of the tube slid easily out of her body, the end of it covered in blood, and the doctor quickly tossed it into the sink. There was very little blood from the insertion spot. He placed a small gauze bandage over the wound, taping it in place, giving us instructions to care for it over the next few days, and we were ready to leave.

Moving Forward

So far we had walked willingly along, not questioning the medical establishment and the societal mantra of "if you can, you should." I mean she had cancer, so you are supposed to do everything you can to fight the disease, no matter how much that destroys you in the process. Isn't that what society tells us, to fight the good fight? And what would family say but that you can beat this.

We had been discussing moving back to Boise where family was after our decision to stop the chemotherapy treatments. Shortly thereafter, my mentor in Boise contacted me and said she was moving back to California, and her position would be open. A couple of quick calls, and they were more than happy to have me back. We quickly arranged for me to transfer back to a position in Boise. Without looking back, Luka and I were on our way heading south, all of our belongings and our animals packed into a U-Haul, leaving behind the green trees and water of Bellingham for the drier landscape of Boise.

We enjoyed a little over a year reprieve from the doctor's visits and the medical procedures before it all started again. While Luka was working at a day care center, an accidental hit to the chest by a child caused a painful bruise. While tending to it and upon close examination, Luka felt a small lump. My heart sunk, and my fear began to dominate me.

After visiting her general practitioner, who felt this was out of her league, a referral came to an oncologist. Following a biopsy, several other tests, X-rays, cat scans, and bone scans we sat in the examining room as the doctor placed X-rays for us to see, showing the golf-ball-sized lump in her left lung.

It was October 13, 1992, when we visited Luka's new oncologist for the results of the biopsy and tests. The doctor took a deep breath and said the small lump in her remaining breast was malignant. "It is cancer."

Hearing the word, we were both thrust back into that nightmare reality once again. She, and I, believed in a better place after this life, heaven, where we would spend eternity, a beautiful place with God and those we loved. However, the fear I now felt overwhelmed those beliefs. I do not want a far better place. I want her, me, us here and now.

Does any of this make sense? The next far better place, are we always searching for that? What is wrong with here? We tell ourselves when a loved one has gone, that they are in a far better place. What does that mean? What solace can we take from that? Is there any? Is this just a Band-Aid on a gaping wound? Is this something that placates us and never really leads to any true healing? So many questions rambled through my mind.

A far better place—the phrase echoes through my mind, and our faith believes this. The words of our God tell us there is a far better place.

Yet I ask, what does that mean, and how do you know? I often want to scream back. Instead, I stood stoically by, a good all-American male raised by hardworking middle-class parents, and nod in a feinted attempt at agreement that there is a far better place.

After so many years and life, my life, has gone on, the world and time moving on. I see the turning of the earth that is often indifferent to the individual joys and sorrows of us who inhabit this planet. In addition, I wondered, my mind forming the question, there is always hope, and hope is never a small thing, right?

CHAPTER 3

Walking Away

Then she turned back to the eternal fountain.
—C. S. Lewis, *A Grief Observed*

Life is a journey they say. It is not about the destination; it is about the journey and the stops along the way from the beginning to the end. Life is one long walk interrupted by small walks that cause us to turn. Sometimes we walk toward something, and sometimes we walk away. Some walks we quickly forget, and others change the direction of our travels and remain with us the rest of our lives.

I had changed my major three times in my first two years of college. I could not decide what I wanted, and everything seemed too big of an adventure for this unsure, quiet, just-turned-twenty-year-old young man. Upon deciding to pursue an art degree, I heard the comments "What will you do with an art degree?" "How will you make a living?" "Are you sure about this?"

With comments ringing in my head meant only to protect me from myself and secure my future, I found myself pursuing a teaching certificate to teach art in junior and senior high schools. It seemed the sensible thing to do, and I mostly seemed to do the sensible and responsible thing. There would always be a need for teachers, and it would give me a chance at making a living. I never knew what "making a living" really meant, only that it was what you are supposed to do—graduate high school, go to college, get a degree, get a job, and become a ghost.

How big and how this decision would affect the rest of my life I had no idea at the time. *Oh my, what had I gotten myself into*, I often thought as the summer turned into fall. The sun still blazed hot in the blue southwestern Idaho sky.

There are those moments in our lives that hold an enchantment, that make our hearts beat faster, filling our senses with excitement and anticipation. The memories remain of what had been, of moments that occurred but then were too quickly gone. Some moments linger, beautiful and tragic in their simplicity, so fleeting and yet they stay with us forever in flawless clarity, a perfect photograph forever hidden in our hearts.

We still recall those lost days and the feelings of anticipation and excitement. It seemed the world had opened up, and the colors, oh my, the colors. The autumn was brilliant in its progression. The leaves on the trees had never been so bright; yellows, reds shone brilliant in the afternoon sun that had slowly burned off the chill from the previous night.

Clear skies of forever blue covered everything uninterrupted, except for an occasional white cloud that slowly drifted by on unseen winds without a care in the world. We sat under those blue skies and told the stories of our lives, and the connection strengthened, two people from different worlds with an invisible thread pulling them closer together toward the future, a future built on hopes and dreams, hopes and dreams shared and held for each other.

Life is truly a journey, one we must all undertake, not knowing what lies around the next bend in the road. In the beginning, it was innocent and pure, just life in the moment full of its joys and sorrow, accomplishments, and minor frustrations. Inconveniences come in life, and this it seemed was one of those. It was after all only a small painful lump in her breast that persisted.

Initial trips to the doctor in Bellingham proved fruitless and uneventful, with initial diagnosis that it could not be serious, assurances that it was nothing to worry about, probably just a cyst or blocked node. The doctors are the experts, the professionals, so when they uttered the *c* word for the first time, that it could not be that because cancerous growths are rarely painful, we hardly batted an eye. Nothing to worry about; it will all be fine. We trusted the establishment, we trusted the system, and what they told us to do, we did. We put our trust in God and trudged forward, listening for words of wisdom.

Because if You Can, You Should

As the days passed, the pain remained and, finally, a biopsy that revealed those dreaded words no one ever wants to hear—a malignant growth. It was breast cancer.

How do you wrap your head around that? Our marriage was only just into its third year when the first diagnosis of cancer came. We were living six hundred miles from any family, and we only had each other. My wife, a young vibrant woman in her midtwenties, a vision with silken hair of dark brown that cascaded down her back, skin a golden tan, and a smile that radiated outward with a joy so profound it immediately touched everyone she met was now fighting for her life.

The words, the recommendations, and major decisions came fast and furious—an ultra-radical mastectomy, then chemotherapy resulting in IV ports and catheters, surgery, hospital stays, endless physicians and nurses, on and on. I found myself dragging through the days soldiering on, taking care of my wife as a dutiful husband because that is what I promised to do because if you can, you should.

We trudged forward, shell-shocked most of the time at what the world had thrown at us. She was the bravest one, always believing that God had a plan. Hope remained our beacon, despite the reality that faced us, although at times, the hope was only a small single candle flame in the dark.

Over the next two and one-half years, life became a show that played out in two very different ways. There was the face we showed the world of young lovers who stood strong and resolute in the face of adversity and probable death, believing in the goodness of a God who would once again resurrect a miracle. We were an example of love on a grand scale, so we believed, and how a loving God would rescue us from the schemes of the enemy and heal Luka. A good God would not allow the destruction of our love, the bonds severed in their infancy, never to be reunited again, would he?

Yet behind the curtain of the stage upon which we played our parts for the world to see, a very different story took place. Rarely do we glimpse behind the curtain, for God only reveals our story to us, not the story of others.

The seemingly endless litany of medical tests—blood draws, X-rays, CAT scans, MRIs, and follow-up appointments to discuss the results—we obligingly complied with while hiding the fear behind the smiles. Our lives revolved around the chemotherapy treatments, radiation, and blood clots that required hospitalization to remedy. There was a brief remission, while unbeknownst to us; cancer had silently continued to spread. When the enemy reared his ugly head again, the c-word was uttered once more, this time metastatic breast cancer.

Almost two years to the day later, cancer had come back with a vengeance, a living thing, I believed, determined more than ever to destroy us. If I could have gotten my hands around it, I would have strangled the life out of it or died trying. However, I could not kill the executioner; I could only tend to her now that she was on death row.

First, it was a growth in Luka's left lung the size of a golf ball. Over the next few months, a spot on the back of her hip appeared and, finally, a spot at the base of her skull up against her spine. The pain, the emotional and physical pain every day that she endured, was immense. The moments of utter despair, the immediacy of the moment drowned out the reality of how this all might eventually play out in the end. It was all Luka could do to get through the days and nights most times, and I did all I could to provide support in whatever way I could. I now found myself on this lonely walk.

As we walked together, she would lean physically on me for support. She walked slowly with an uneven gait. Old before her time, she hobbled, similar to someone three times her age, answering honestly when asked if she had hurt her leg. She would reply, "Yes, I have cancer." Most who had ventured to ask the question would not know what to say to her reply. They would stand astonished at her brash boldness, mumble a condolence, quickly turn and walk away. Luka never said this with bitterness or anger in her voice. I admired her bold honesty in facing the truth she lived each day. She walked upon this road as she was the one dying.

Behind the drawn shades and locked doors in the evenings and nights, Luka sometimes wailed and cried over the pain. The prescribed morphine lessened the physical pain but caused so many hallucinations that she often did not know what world she was living in. These episodes scared me to my core. I was seeing through her eyes beyond the physical to the realm of the spiritual.

I did what I could around the house by cooking, cleaning, doing the laundry, and chauffeuring her around. I helped her dress, get up out of the chair, helped as she limped to the bathroom, helped her off the toilet, and so many other small seemingly inconsequential things. All through our time together, we had taken walks through the neighborhoods wherever we happened to be living, talking, laughing, and sometimes just being together in silence. Now that was over. Time together was the only thing, just being with her, sitting talking, watching movies, and holding her hand, so many things that I now believe may have helped her breathe a little easier in those moments.

There were long endless nights when she could not sleep because of the physical pain and the emotional anguish. We sat in the hot tub for hours, the buoyancy of the water alleviating the ache by taking the weight off her body until our skin was pruned and white. Watching movies together into the wee hours of the morning are special memories of moments we shared together. We often talked late into the night and early morning, of what I have no recollection, and we often just sat quietly, her head on my shoulder as I held her close.

The Path Less Taken

The days passed as winter faded up to that last afternoon in the hospital on a bright sunny spring day in April. This long walk, interspersed by so many side trails and experiences, seemed close to the end. The final trail marker indicating the summit was just up ahead. What else could I do? Was all hope now gone?

Now I stood at her hospital bedside displaying an outward calm, holding her hand and occasionally whispering and singing softly into her ear. Everything around me faded into silence as her breath was shallow, raspy, and barely audible. Her eyes stared blankly toward the ceiling, her lids half closed, her body still. Yet I believed in those moments and still do now that she could hear my voice and understand my words.

What do you see, my love? I wanted to ask. What is beyond? Do you see where you are going? Do you understand what is happening? Are you aware of this moment? I kept my questions to myself and simply stayed in this ultimate moment of transcendence where life and death meet in a final embrace before we each jump from the summit, alone.

I stood, my feet rooted to the spot where I stood at her side; this walk was not over yet. Wild horses could not drag me away, and I was unable to leave even if I had wanted to, and yet hating every single second I was there. I could do nothing. All I had done before now had come down to this. This helplessness filled with me with hopelessness, every fiber of my being, and I could not, would not, walk away. As she breathed her last, her unmoving eyes stared into eternity, I stood silently, barely breathing, and I wanted to run as far away as I could get from the reality that had unfolded around me.

With a trembling hand, I reached over and gently placed my fingertips on the soft skin of her lids and closed them over her lifeless blue eyes. After several minutes that seemed an eternity, I do not know how long, I released my grip on her hand and laid it gently on the bed at her side. I straightened up and stepped slowly back from the bed as if she were something dangerous and to be feared. I stared at her lifeless body, before me a once-vibrant woman who now lay still.

There is nothing in the world that can prepare you for the emptiness that a life leaves behind. I was suddenly a widower at twenty-eight years old, something I had never ever even considered. Is not that a fate reserved for those who have loved into old age, a love that has lasted across the years? Not for young adults, right, especially after such a short marriage? But that was a path that I now must walk.

Small sounds marked the uncomfortable silence in the room, soft weeping, heavy breathing, clearing of throats, and the scuffling of feet as others nervously shifted their weight. Through the fog, I heard a soft voice and a hand on my arm, "Do you want to get out of here?" I barely nodded. Guided out of the hospital room, no one spoke, down the hallway, to the elevators, across the hospital lobby, out the doors into the brightness of the late afternoon sun, and across the parking lot where I ended up standing by the cars in silence.

There were no words spoken. There was nothing to say. My mind was reeling with the final reality of all of this, yet numb to the emotion. No tears fell from my eyes. Walking away from her lifeless body, from the hope we had, was the longest walk of my young life.

Looking back, I wonder what I thought in those moments. What do you do when the waves of finality wash over you and cover you in a different reality? Can one single moment define your entire life? A life is made up of a series of events, some happy, some sad, some magic, and some tragic. The tragic moments, the events filled with trauma, pain, and loss irrevocably change us forever. There is no going back from these events. We are undeniably not the same as we were before, so the question remains—what do you do with that?

The path before me was now an open book with empty pages. Here I was, months before my twenty-ninth birthday, and a long, unknown, and open future in front me, a map with no directions. I was lost at sea with no wind in my sails. I had the freedom to do, to be, to go anywhere I wanted, and I did not want that freedom. I was free to walk away. How do you reconcile that?

CHAPTER 4

Still Miles to Walk

Dying is not what happens to you.
Dying is what you do.
—Stephen Jenkinson, *Die Wise:*
A Manifesto of Serenity and Soul

She had suffered and died. The end of her life here on earth also marked the end of so many other things. No matter what you believe, there are so many things that will never be again. It is nonnegotiable, undeniable, and chaotic. Then it hits you; there are so many things still to do, different things, walks down paths you chose to believe never existed, and if they did, you would somehow avoid ever traveling them.

I found myself standing in a small little room before a wooden pine casket. I had picked out this casket because it was more natural looking, and the manufacturer promised to plant a tree in honor of the deceased. A nice gesture, I thought, and Luka would have liked it; she loved the outdoors. Now standing in this little room in front of the casket that contained the body of my dead wife, I wanted to be anywhere but here. It was to the moment almost exactly three days, seventy-two hours, since she had died.

Earlier that day, I had stood in front of our closet staring at her clothes hanging there, clothes she would never wear again. The surreal reality of the moment was overwhelming, and I only was able to move thanks to the support of others that were there with me at that time. Tonight was the viewing at the funeral home, the day before the service.

The funeral home asked us to bring a picture of Luka, a recent one, so they could use that to apply her makeup. As we were both artists ourselves, I found it an interesting concept that now some stranger would use their "artistic" talents to apply makeup to her corpse, and she would then lay on display for others to see. Dying requires so much of us, even after we are dead.

I had gone through the stack of pictures one by one. Her face in each photograph brought up so many conflicting emotions. This was all I had left of her, and I pushed down the pain and the anguish, wearing my stoicism like a badge of honor. The funeral home employees were extremely gracious during this time. This bizarre ritual of dressing up the dead for others to look at baffled me, a shell of a person, just a body, all primped and pressed, with a painted-on face laid out for all to see in a human-size breadbox.

Driving back to the funeral home, I could barely feel my body, and I could not remember ever being this tired. Even during the months of caring for Luka and the late nights, early mornings, and all the tasks, I could not remember being this tired.

For then there was a purpose; I was caring for her and helping her. Now there seemed no purpose to my days. I was just doing the obligatory things the world tells you and expects you to do after someone dies, the responsible and sensible things. It did not matter what I did now; it would not bring Luka back, no matter what. We had crossed the line, and that was not a finish line, for there was no finish line that I could see and no awakening from this nightmare that was now my life.

Protecting Her Even in Death

I wanted to run. I wanted to scream, but I could only move forward, dutifully fulfilling the obligations and responsibilities that confronted me. There was no escape, so I slowly approached the casket. Those accompanying lingered back in silence. The first thing I noticed was that the lipstick color they had applied to her lips was out of place and wrong, a color she would have never been caught dead wearing, pun intended, and now here she lay dead, with hideous orange-reddish-colored lipstick painted on her lips.

I felt my knees buckle. My breath caught in my throat. Her lips were all I could see. Those same lips that I had kissed on so many occasion now looked like bright-orange earthworms on her face. The anger welled up inside like a tidal wave. My mind reeled, and I spoke aloud, saying over and over, "No, no, no! This is not her, and this is not going to work! The lipstick is too orange and not the right color!"

I was furious, saddened, and confused all at the same time. It felt like my one last attempt to protect her, to allow her to keep her dignity intact even in death, had failed.

The embarrassed funeral home employees quickly apologized. There was still time to rectify this they said. I stood; my anguish mixed with such confusion. They had said nothing about bringing makeup with the clothes. My anger fumed for how was I to know. I had never done this before.

Many were so accommodating in my time of sorrow, and my outburst was swallowed in gratitude. My emotions swayed from gratitude for those helping and the anger that I had to see to these things and make decisions.

It was after five-thirty, and she was now ready for the public viewing scheduled to begin at seven o'clock. *This is not happening*, I kept telling myself as we walked out of the funeral home.

I could not stay and had no intention of hanging around the funeral home to accept condolences from family, friends, and strangers in front of her dead body. I ended up that evening driving around Boise with Luka's younger brother who had just arrived from out of town. We drove, and we talked.

I felt obligated to be there for him, again stuffing my own pain and assuming the role of "what can I do for you." Always the caregiver? I dropped him off and drove through the quiet streets of Boise to our house as the sky was darkening into the night.

Going Home

I opened the door and walked into the little house Luka and I called home. A cold darkness hit and washed over me as I walked into the empty house. The late evening light came through the windows, casting eerie shadows across the floor. After being gone for most of the day, the dog and cats seemed glad; someone was home. Nevertheless, all I felt was the chill of early spring evening.

I felt the aloneness wash over me, agitated at the little boy that I felt rise up inside of me. On autopilot, I filled the cat dishes with food. Then I stood in the middle of the kitchen holding the food scoop.

Tomorrow is the funeral, I thought to myself, *a day I am dreading*. I stood in the stillness of the house, confused at how I had gotten to this point. I thought further that how could it be any worse than what I have already experienced. I needed out of the house; the air felt suffocating. Getting my feet to move, I grabbed a cold beer from the fridge and headed for the back door.

RC, our little dog, dashed through the door, glad to be outside. I closed the screen door behind me as both cats came over, sitting down on the other side where they stared out into the night. I sat down on the back steps and took a long slow drink of the beer as I watched the spring night sky turn a darker blue, and the twinkling stars began to appear overhead.

I did not want her to be on display, and I did not want to be on display myself. My anger rose into a fury at the pity I felt from others. It was hard for me to accept. As I sipped on the beer, the night closed in around me, and I hid in the darkness. I felt the cold chilly April night, and all I knew was I wanted to turn back the hands of time.

I felt caught in a world that no longer made sense, and I wondered, *Did it ever really make sense, or are we just fooling ourselves*.

While she was alive, although the cancer was ravaging her body, we still had hope and each other. A smile, the touch of a hand, a warm embrace, or a simple I love you could steady you with a hope, even for the moment, a belief that you could face whatever might come, together.

I was not sure what to do with that hope now. It seemed a poor substitute, a hope of a reunion someday on some far distant shore in the hereafter. I wanted her now, her physical presence next to me, a warm hand to hold, not this vision of a delicately painted porcelain doll that now lay perfectly placed in a wooden box. Tomorrow, others would flock to a church where she would lay inside that box.

I continued to sip my beer. I watched as the night sky turned darker, and more stars appeared overhead. My voice split the silence of the night as I stared up into the blackness and asked, "Are you up there, Luka?"

There came no reply as I sat on the steps. The minutes ticked by, and the memories flooded my mind as the tears began to fall. They streamed down my face, for the first time since Saturday night and only the second time since she had died. I buried my head in my arms across my knees and cried as RC came up to me and gently licked my arms with his soft wet tongue.

Tomorrow Comes

As sure as the turning of the earth, the next day dawned. It was a typical spring day in southern Idaho; high clouds crossed the blue backdrop of sky as the sun played its typical game of hide-and-seek. The temperature was normal for this time of year, comfortable with a slight breeze.

The church was beautiful; a plethora of flowers adorned the stage and surrounded the wooden casket. Although I was mostly oblivious to the gracious support of others, there was a long line of blessings from those who surrounded me at this time. I was numb, and all I could think was she—her lifeless body—was lying there in that box up in front for all to see, a freak show of epic proportions that so-called civilized society deemed acceptable, and it all seemed so wrong. They say men can compartmentalize easier than women, compartmentalize and shut down their emotions. Well, on this day, if there was a contest, I would have been crowned champion of the world.

As the church filled with mourners, family, and friends, many I did not know, the air filled with expectancy, a sense of hope and sorrow. Family members and I were led to the front-row pews just before the service began. After taking our seats, the upbeat contemporary Christian song "Five Smooth Stones" by Bryan Duncan blared over the church' speaker system.

I had specifically chosen it to start the service, despite some curious looks from others. The song had become one of Luka's favorites during the past few months, and it gave her hope and courage. When the song ended, the pastor approached the microphone, and his first words with a chuckle were "Well, now that everyone is awake, on behalf of the families I would like to welcome you…" I heard the quiet laughter at the pastor's opening remark.

I then stopped listening as I smiled inside, knowing that Luka would be happy at that. She always enjoyed surprising people, and I had stressed to the pastor during our meeting that this funeral would not be the sorrowful, boring affair that seemed to follow the deaths of many people. No matter how much I was hurting, this was going to be a celebration of a young woman who had fought her hardest against the disease, and she deserved better because she always believed there was hope.

The service continued in a more traditional sense from there. Accompanied to the lectern by my sister, my voice shook as I read a pathetic poem I had written for the occasion. My hands shook, my legs were unsteady all the way through, until I finally returned to my seat. I sat unmoving, stoic and barely hearing the sermon through the rest of the service. My only thought as the preacher droned on was that he should wrap this up because if Luka had been here, she would be getting antsy about now because this was taking too long.

I sat in the front row on the aisle, unmoving with my head down as person after person passed me making their way toward the front of the church. Most were silent, lost in their own thoughts I assumed, and honestly, I did not care. Occasionally, there was a soft touch on my shoulder as they went forward. Head down, I watched the legs of each as they each passed by the casket in slow procession, saying their own personal final goodbyes. I was lost in disoriented memories of my own when I was shaken out of my reverie as a hand slapped me hard on the back.

I looked up; my face not revealing my surprise. I saw an older man I did not know slowly passing me by. His hard hand on my back had startled me, and whether he had lost his balance and fell into me or just unaware of how hard he had slapped me I will never know. I came back to the present and realized that he was one of the last people in the line to proceed forward. I sat and sank back into myself, unaware of those few still around me.

The last few people passed by the casket. Family got up and paid their respects, and I sat, not knowing what to do. Crap, I had never done this before. What was my role here? Is there etiquette or protocol that I was supposed to follow? I had been winging this for months, even years now. Ever since Luka had been diagnosed the first time, through all the treatments, her dying, and right up to this point as the funeral service ended, I had been making this up as I went along. And I still didn't know what to do.

The funeral home director was suddenly at my side, and he quietly said, "We have cleared the church, if you'd like to spend a few moments alone with her."

Oh my god, I thought. This is really it. I could not speak, only nodded my head in acknowledgment. He turned and walked toward the back of the church as I sat unable to move. After many seconds, the church filled with a silence that was deafening. I slowly stood and stared at the wooden casket a mere ten feet or so in front of me where her body lay. I stood and approached slowly and stood next to the casket, my eyes dry. I felt as if I had no tears to cry. Besides, I reminded myself boys don't cry in front of others, especially cowboys.

I stared down at her, remembering her smile, her laughter, the way her eyes sparkled, and the love that she showed when alive. Her love was a real and living force that moved people and left ripples wherever she went. Now she lay, eyes closed, still, silent, and cold.

Over the past three days, so many people talked about her as if she was no more, but here she was, lying in front of me. I remembered a young girl, smiling, who I had long ago wed.

I pulled a single red rose from the bouquet lying at the end of the casket and laid it gently at the bend of her right elbow. Her were hands clasped, resting lightly on her stomach. This was my wife, my love, my friend, my future, and my hope that lay still before me.

With no forethought, I placed my hands on the edge of the casket and leaned forward ever so gently as my face approached hers, and I softly kissed those now cold dead red lips. They were those same lips that I had kissed so many times before, lips that had stirred up emotions and passions in my mind and body time and time again. This time there was no response, just a flat hard numbness. I stood upright, still staring down into the casket before turning away as I felt the thunder of my heartbreak again.

My legs moved on their own as I strode down the center aisle of the church between the now-empty pews on either side. My cowboy boots made soft sounds on the carpeted floor. Ignoring those still gathered in the foyer, I quickly walked, striding by the remaining family and friends. Their voices quieted as they saw my approach, and I avoided making eye contact.

The midafternoon sun was now in high swing. Exiting the church, I immediately turned right, down the sidewalk, and turned right again when I reached the edge of the building. I walked along the side of the building and to the back parking lot behind the church and sat down on a curb, my knees up to my chest, and I stared at the pavement in front of me. No tears fell as I thought of the last few minutes of my life, that last kiss and walking away, knowing that there were still miles to walk on this road, and it was just beginning.

CHAPTER 5

Death Is Only the Beginning

The Young Girl That I Long Ago
Wed and Who Drove Me Mad
—Mark Wayne

The young girl that I long ago wed
Promising to love and cherish
Until death do us part
There was truth in those words I said

It was another lifetime in another place when she stood next to me in a world that does not exist anymore. Before God, family, and friends I promised to "love and cherish until death do us part." Looking back and recalling the memories, I never realized the supreme truth of those words when I spoke them, to keep my vows in the face of tests time after time over the next few short years. There were so many challenges that continually pushed me to my breaking point and often beyond. Love is excruciatingly hard at times, and nothing prepares you for that.

The young girl I held safe in my arms
When she cried from hurt
While our love grew
I attempted to shield her from harm

My arms were not enough to protect her and keep her safe when she cried from the hurt and fear. Falling in love was easy, and I vowed to shield her from harm as any man would do for the one he loved. I was young and naïve, believing with all my heart that I could fix whatever came our way. I promised to stand in the gap and take each fiery dart the enemy could throw at us.

The young girl who held nothing back
We feasted on love and lust
Unaware fate conspired
To cleave two souls and fade to black

She loved me in return, holding nothing back in beautiful moments of our youth when we feasted on our love and lust. The early days drifted on towards a wide-open and unknown future in front of us. We were unaware fate conspired against us, eventually separating and leaving us both alone to face the black.

The young girl who endured the pain
Of the cancerous disease that arose
A future uncertain
And rarely did she ever complain

I have heard it said that life is pain, and if they tell you otherwise, they are trying to sell you something. Cynical perhaps, but I watched her endure the tremendous pain from the cancerous disease that began and coursed through her young body. It ravaged her mind, racking her emotionally as it devastated her once-youthful figure and psyche. The future became immensely uncertain, and rarely did I hear her protest.

The young girl in a faithful anguish
Moments of joy midst affliction
As her star began to fade
A beautiful life now left to languish

Helpless, I watched as time marched on, and each day became harder than the one before. She continued to smile, treasuring the small moments of joy amid this most serious of afflictions. I could see her star begin to fade, a beautiful life left to languish in uncertainty while her faith grew stronger in her tender young heart.

The young girl I gently held her hand
Watching as life slowly slipped away
Until her last breath
And it was all I could do to stand

The days rolled on, multiplying to a short five and one-half years, until before me, she silently lay in the stark coldness of a hospital room, her life slowly slipping away. I watched, holding my breath, until she slowly took her last, and it was all I could do to stand, while everything screamed to run. It was then that time in my heart stopped, while all else around me continued to turn.

The young girl I gently closed her eyes
No more sight and nothing to see
Worlds she now explores
With eyes that went blank when she died

At the last and with my trembling fingers, I reached toward her, gently closing her eyes for there was no more sight and nothing left to see. In a moment of grace, she was gone. I wonder still to this day what worlds she now explores with those beautiful blue eyes that went blank when she died.

The young girl from whom I slowly turned away
My heart beat loud as I silently wept
The long walk leaving behind
Every dream gone and I could not stay

I slowly turned away as my heart beat loudly, and inside I silently wept. I began the longest walk of my young life, leaving behind every dream, for I knew I could not stay. I prayed that she would arrive safely at heaven's door. Scars and all, she had fought the good fight, yet still for me, there was more.

The young girl is now just a lifeless shell
All the memories a distant reverie
My heart now shattered
Knowing that I have entered hell

She lay before me now, just an empty husk, the years fading into this nightmare I would never forget. My heart now shattered into a million pieces of jagged glass that all the king's horses and all the king's men could not put back together again, for I knew my path had entered hell.

The young girl lies tranquil in a wooden box
All prettied up in peaceful repose
Her struggle now done
A life put away in a human breadbox

Her body, now dead and stiff, fitted neatly inside a pine wooden box. They prettied her up as if for a night on the town. She had no worries anymore; her struggle now forever done some would say, another lost and expendable life put away like a loaf of bread in a human box.

The young girl lay for everyone to see
A lifeless corpse is all that is left
My strength now gone
Sitting front and center is killing me

She lay still in the box, unable to rise and leave. Her dead body lay on display for onlookers to see so each could slake their morbid curiosity. She left behind only an unresponsive shell, her choices now all taken from her. I could no longer protect her, my own strength now gone, and having to sit here in the church pew is a peculiar kind of torture.

> The young girl lies while they all file past
> Alone I stare into the dark void
> My hopes now taken
> The answer was no to each prayer I asked

They all slowly filed past, some known and some not. I cared not what they thought for I was lost in the fog of my thoughts. Sitting alone, I stared into the dark void in front of me. My hopes for the future were now taken, and all I could think was, *God why would you say the answer was no to each prayer I asked?*

> The young girl towards her I slowly reach out
> Placing a single red rose upon her chest
> Those red lips I kissed
> They are cold and stiff she is gone no doubt

As it ends, I cautiously approached, each horror movie where the body does rise dancing through my mind. I stood before the body of my dead wife and slowly reached. The delicate red rose I lay upon her chest. Leaning down I found myself falling into the darkness of loss and regret. Her red lips I gently kissed; they are stone now, cold and stiff. She is gone; of this, I have no doubt.

> The young girl to ashes and dust she returns
> The small container I must carry away
> Life's arc from birth to death
> In the light of time she will forever burn

Out of ashes we were formed; out of the dark we were born. To ashes and dust, she has now returned. A small canister I hold in my hands. Inside, it contains all that is left of a once and future life. It seems just another sad story of the inevitability of each life's arc from birth to death. Somewhere on the wings of the spring afternoon breeze I hear angels singing, and I so want to believe that now she had broken the bonds and fallen into eternity's embrace.

> The young girl I take over land and sea afar
> To a place where the waters are alive
> Calling forth another life
> A dance beckons journeying to the stars

The time has come to take another road, traveling through the air to a place far away. Into the midnight sun I go, where neither of us has ever ventured before. I hope that this act of staring into eternity gives her wings to join the dance of a thousand stars.

> The young girl now flies free in the slipstream
> Her ashes spread to eternity's embrace
> Promises kept of a dying wish
> Into the undiscovered now just a dream

Each piece floats away on wind and water, disappearing into the mist. Her body now offered in forever gratitude to eternity's embrace, letting go to fulfill a wish. If you love something, set it free. It was an act to hold true to promises kept of a dying wish so she continues her voyage into the undiscovered, and am I now just a dream?

> The young girl who left me a wandering nomad
> I carry hope of once and a future again
> I chose the reality of love
> And the young girl who drove me mad

I can still travel back to another time, place, and hold the memories of her who so innocently left me adrift. I had no anchor to stall my wandering through my youth. I traversed the valley's path alone; now the hope I have carried gives me a future again, for long ago, I chose the reality of love which left me with the memories of a young girl who drove me mad.

Madness Reigns

After someone dies, now that they are dead, do they often cease to be our dead? Are they simply the dead instead? They are no longer ours, not really, if they ever were, and I felt suddenly that I now came from nowhere. No one sees the many things of grief behind the curtain. Until we are in that moment for ourselves, they are but a shadow that dances around the edges of our minds. All those little things from a life lived together, some meaningful and important, some not, but each one can bring the pangs of grief red-hot when one least expects it. There is nothing to do but to endure and hang onto the memories and the pain until it begins to fade.

Another lifetime ago, I stood silently holding the hand of someone I planned to spend the rest of my life with as they lay dying. Feeling entirely helpless, I could only watch her die from the evil cancer that ravaged her young body. I have traversed my own valley of shadows, and occasionally, I will wander and find myself back there in that dark. I have cried, screamed, railed, and bargained against the seeming injustice of it all and the randomness of another beautiful life gone. I pitied myself while many tried to show me compassion, kindness, and tenderness.

I have slowly realized over the years that my own pain should not and must not be the focus. Every person is fighting a battle, and most of us have no idea. I know that many I have encountered over the years never see my scars for I carry them on the inside. The pain hidden deep, I retreat like a frightened child.

Can you live a lifetime in five short years? Who can define a lifetime for others? To each it is unique. Five years, ten years, twenty, thirty, fifty, or more, a lifetime is what one makes of it. Does the joy and sorrow experienced echo in eternity? From life to death and back to life, my journey has taken me there. Life goes on; we do not get that choice. We can only choose whether we engage in it or not.

It only matters what we do with our lives, each second, minute, hour, and days that add up to a lifetime. Sometimes we have years or decades, and sometimes a lifetime here is so much shorter. The memories we carry, and we speak of the dead as if they once were and are no more, but is that right?

Luka spent her last day on earth drugged on pain medicine and sleeping, rather dying, through most of the day. It was shortly after four o'clock in the afternoon that she took her last breath. At the time, I was numb, and it all just seemed so wrong, so anticlimactic, if you will. *So this was it*, I thought. *No trumpets, no angels singing halleluiah, no bright light, no...nothing. She was just gone.*

Her death was a massive jolt to my reality no earthquake could match. It shook every corner of my world and tilted it on its axis, sending it spinning wildly out of control, although at first, I felt none of it. It was only a bad dream I just needed to wake up and shake it off. Everything I had ever come to know now skewed in a world of hurt, pain, malaise, and confusion.

I walked through the ensuing days of overwhelming fog where each thought only echoed forever in my brain, while my body followed the course of least resistance. The voices seemed so far away, and the reasons why eluded me as only a sense of duty and fulfilling the obligations kept me moving forward.

Looking back, I see myself a young man of twenty-eight years, innocent to the immense reality of life and death that go hand in hand, innocent, naive, and unprepared for the path that I now walked. How can we be so surprised when someone dies when everybody already knows we all are going to die?

At the last moments, two soft hands were gently tearing us apart, pulling us in opposite directions. I can see now that my mind knew what was happening. Two young hearts had come together, and now the inevitable parting was before us. She had now traveled to an unknown world beyond this life, leaving me with a life with the same adornments around, the same locations, same people, the responsibilities, and me—but without her.

It would be months before the fog lifted for any length of time where I could see somewhat clearly. It was years of madness and riding away before I could put together coherent thoughts about my experience. My thoughts have struggled to weave the seemingly unrelated events of a life into a whole that has resulted in this book because death is only the beginning.

CHAPTER 6

To Love What's Leaving

He could only stand silently, as
he watched her fading.
—Mark Wayne

I have read many books about grief and loss on my journey of healing and during my research for this book. Some were from the perspective of those who have lost a loved one suddenly. Different paths prior to death than my own, they still evoke memories of the long journey Luka and I were on from the moment we met. I learned very early in our relationship that she had cancer as a youngster, and I knew there was a probability that it could return. There was always the possibility of a relapse, and she most likely would never be able to have children.

Studies have shown that depending on the amount of radiation therapy received and chemotherapy regimen used that female survivors of Hodgkin lymphoma have an increased risk of breast cancer. In addition, once breast cancer occurs, there is a higher risk of dying from said breast cancer than compared to those with no history of Hodgkin lymphoma.

I knew none of this until after she died. Would it have changed anything? No, none of these possibilities would have stopped me from falling in love and wanting to spend my life with her. We were married after two years of dating seriously and began our life of husband and wife together. The first two years of our marriage together were the typical honeymoon phase of blessings and thinking about what the future might bring. We were focused on and only thinking about the good things that were in our future together.

She was diagnosed with breast cancer in the fall of 1990, possibly a mastitis from the Hodgkin's lymphoma she had has as a child, and then she died just two and one-half years later. We lived with the cloud of her disease hanging over us, like an unwelcome guest that will not leave, from the beginning of our relationship. Following the initial diagnosis, the uninvited guest took up permanent residence. We had no choice but rarely acknowledged the reality.

Stephen Jenkinson, in his book *Die Wise*, says loving someone is not inevitable; loving someone who will die is. Loving someone who will die is human work. I look back now, knowing what I know now and did not know then, and I would not have taken a different path.

The pain of losing someone never goes away, and you never get over it; you carry it with you. In my situation, as each day went by, I was watching my wife slowly die. We are all dying day by day, but following the diagnosis, I instinctively knew death would find her, statistically, probably before me, and it happened much sooner than I had ever imagined.

Living with Dying

We did not talk about the end, and we did not plan for her death. We did not make funeral arrangements together or talk about how I would go on without her. Call us immature or unwilling to face a possible reality, whatever. No one briefed us on the proper way to handle what life had thrown at us.

We missed the class on how to die, what it asks of us, and what it could all mean. This may have been a built-in mechanism to shield our minds from the reality, whether we were in denial, or we just did not believe that this would be how it would all play out.

We simply lived our lives each day, loving one another and doing what we could. The ever-growing cancer in her body eventually made her weaker and weaker day after day. Being so close to her, I often failed to see this gradual transition until the very end. Then life forced me to acknowledge how sick she was. Again maybe this was denial. So many years later, I still do not know for sure. She was my wife, my friend, everything I wanted, and everything I needed. I could not accept the hard truth, to believe that right before my eyes, each day Luka was dying a little. While I prayed for a miracle and more time with her, she suffered more each day in the midst of the ongoing process of dying.

The reality of life, a life that often sucked, that I lived each day was waking each morning to face the pain and helplessness of another day watching her die, even if I could not speak those words aloud. I see now looking back that she was dying just like a plant that is not watered. Her body began to wither ever so slowly and surely a little more each day.

Every morning I arose, I had to face a new day, another day I had to endure and hold my pain at her suffering, another day to watch her die. When the sun set every night or when I went to sleep, I prayed for relief, not for me but for her, only to find that each tomorrow would bring another day where I could do little but watch her die.

We go through our days, especially as men, hiding behind so many masks, and almost imperceptibly, piece by piece, day by day, little by little, and moment by moment, over the years…there is nothing left, and our soul dies. They will tell you what to do, who to be, and what to say. So I ask, who are they, and why do we listen to them anyway? We feel it is not right but allow ourselves to stray from our truth, losing our authenticity. We go through life in a daze hiding in our strength, never letting them see us cry and then, there is simply this:

"Jesus wept."

It is the shortest verse in the Bible, John 11:35. Is this a weakness, a failing, a lack of...something? Can we truly love and care for another with no ulterior motives? Only when we acknowledge our own fears and failures can we even begin to offer some of the better parts of ourselves. You have exactly what you need, and someone needs what you have to give. Acknowledge your fears, feel the sadness, celebrate the joys, love others relentlessly, believe in hope, grab hold of life, and never let go. Live in wonder, in fascination of things, knowing that you will be devastated in the end.

Our life was normal in most respects, other than Luka had this disease growing inside her body during most of our marriage. In the springtime, we planted flowers and a garden that we tended all summer long. Luka loved the outdoors and her yard, and we loved making it look pretty and inviting through many simple landscaping projects. We tore out concrete and put in a stepping-stone walkway, prepared beds and planted flowers, rototilled a spot for a garden, and built a compost bin.

From our first meeting in an art class, there was always the art, paintings, drawings, and something creative going on, including making live green centerpieces during the holiday season to both give to friends and family and sell at holiday bazaars. All the while, she was fighting this battle, and the exhaustion was a constant companion. It is hard work, living while you are dying, and hard to love someone you know is leaving.

I suppose it played tricks on her mind also. Her moods would swing up and down. Luka's passion for life would be full and vibrant one minute and then angry and melancholy the next. She could explode without warning, often directed at me. I would often cower from her anger as it escalated. I felt trapped, and the fights that ensued would be epic.

We both said things we later regretted, but we both knew we were in it for the long haul. She once slapped me across the face after a remark I made regarding her emotional fidelity. Although I do not remember the exact words said, the slap she landed hard on the side of my face my memory recalls. I can still see the tears streaming from her blue eyes and down her checks as she stood staring at me. In the words of Captain Jack Sparrow (Johnny Depp), "I deserved that."

Being Useful When Death Comes

There were always animals in the house. Luka's love for her furry family was evident, and they became her surrogate children, the ones we never had. She doted on the animals and loved them passionately. There was RC, my little white dog, a cocker poodle mix that I had before Luka and I got together. He became the mainstay and our third companion during our relationship and the many adventures we had.

There were other animals in the short time we were together. I remember the brief time of some, and one that sticks out in my mind is Pearls, the little white kitty Luka had when she lived with some friends before we were married. Pearls disappeared one night, and we eventually found she had been picked up by the Humane Society after being hit by a car. I remember bringing home the body of Pearls, this small little cat, so we could bury her. Holding a large brown paper bag, I opened it slowly to show Luka the body of Pearls lying curled at the bottom, looking like she was asleep. Again, why are we so surprised when someone or something dies? It is supposed to happen, and the shattering happens to us right on schedule.

Later, we inherited two black kittens from somewhere I no longer recall, a brother and sister. Sly was the tall lanky all-black male, and his little sister, Koshka, was a little ball of black fur with reddish tints on the end of her long hairs. Sly and Luka became inseparable, and Koshka, more of a loner, became my cat by default. She was still a little sweetheart and so lovable, and Luka loved them both.

Later, we also had a large Siamese cat named Kahlua, who weighed close to seventeen pounds. She was a cat that nothing seemed to faze, also a real loner who loved to be outside. The three cats got along well together, and RC was often the odd one out being the only dog of the mix, but he was the one that thoroughly enjoyed partaking in the car rides and excursions.

After Luka died, I had RC, Sly, Koshka, and Kahlua who would wander the house looking for her, especially Sly, meowing and crying. It brought me up short every time for I knew he was looking for her. I think they all knew, Sly more than the others did, that she would not be coming back. Grief was everywhere in the house, and each of us was navigating it the best we could.

As time rolls on, and death claims each living thing, the animals are now just memories, as is Luka, memories I carry with me and always will. Sly and Kahlua both died of old age, and maybe some heartache and loneliness led them to an earlier death than might have been if things were different; who really knows. They were each a lifeline to Luka for me to hold onto, and as each one, left the line between Luka, them, and me has become thinner and thinner.

There is the remorse and guilt I still feel from that fateful day in July, three months after Luka's death, when I rolled and crashed my car in which RC disappeared. I talk in detail about this in a later chapter. I live with the feeling that it was my actions that killed him, however accidental. My memories of the accident are dim and fractured; thus, I have questions that still haunt me to this day.

I have especially vivid memories of Koshka's death, how she was the next one to leave this world after Luka's death later that summer following my vehicle rollover accident. I remember coming home one summer evening, and I heard a wailing meow coming from the garage. Opening the garage door, I found Koshka lying on the cement floor in a corner of the garage. Her soft little eyes looked at me as she cried again, more quietly this time. I immediately could tell she been hurt, although I could see no sign of external injuries. I bent down, and I gently picked her up, carried her to the passenger seat of the car, gently laying her down.

I took her to the emergency vet in town who was open late. After an examination and tests, they said there was nothing they could do. She had broken bones and internal injuries, so I made the gut-wrenching decision to have her put down. Marking another death in the span of a few short months, I watched as they injected her, and this little ball of fur that I loved slowly stopped breathing and lay completely still. I stared unemotional and remembered the body of Luka lying still in the hospital bed months before, lifeless.

I took Koshka's little body in a cardboard box back home where I retrieved a shovel from the same garage where I had found her earlier. I grabbed a six-pack of beer and headed for the desert as the sky was beginning to darken. This was something I had to do and something I had to do alone. I headed out, telling no one where I was headed, what I was doing, and that was how I wanted it.

By the time I reached the immense span of desert and the area where Luka and I had been many times before, the night was almost completely upon the land. It was dark, a few stars appearing in the dark summer sky overhead. My headlights were flashing up and down across the sagebrush as my vehicle bounced down the dirt road of the southwestern Idaho desert.

I found a spot and parked, turning off the engine, and cracking open a beer, I started drinking. The dark sky above continued to fill with a multitude of twinkling lights over my head. The dark sky felt suffocating as the coldness of the beer washed down my throat. What the next step was I knew, but I lingered in the silence of the night, far away from the city lights and the throngs of humanity.

Taking a deep breath, I set down the beer can and retrieved the small box where Koshka's dead body lay. I grabbed the shovel, and carrying it and the box with me, I walked slowly, looking for a spot that felt right. It was extremely dark so far from the city lights, and I walked slowly. I knew that I would have to turn and walk away once it was finished.

I found a spot and began digging a hole to place the box into. The dirt was hardpan clay with rocks, and the digging was slow. Upon finishing, I was sweating and wiping the perspiration from my brow. I placed the box gingerly into the hole, whispered a goodbye, and began shoveling dirt on top. The sound of the dirt and rocks made an eerie thudding sound as it hit the top of the cardboard box. The sound echoed across the quiet of the desert night. I patted down the fresh earth as best I could before placing several large rocks over the spot to hopefully keep it undisturbed for as long as possible.

I whispered another little prayer of goodbye to Koshka before returning to the car and driving away. I left her there alone and felt even more alone as well, something I did not think was possible. It was one more life lost, one more instance of the reality of love. As I drove back toward the city lights, leaving the vast dark emptiness behind, my heart carried an unending emptiness inside. This theme that the things I loved I was losing one by one reminded me that each one of us will be leaving this world also. It was another notch in the bedpost of life marking another death, and I felt even more alone.

Days dragged on, and my hollow life continued as the summer dragged on. Sly knew his little sister was gone, and the house became even emptier than before. Each life that left created new holes that nothing would fill. I stood often staring at the picture on the refrigerator door of Luka holding Sly, and they both looked so happy and content. I would often hold Sly as he slept on my lap, which made me feel a little better and closer to those I had lost. Although I knew that eventually, my memories of him also would be the only connection left between us. I did not understand the grief. My heart was broken and yet, I never wanted it to mend.

CHAPTER 7

I Am the One Dying

Because the things I am believing are only a dream,
or because I only dream that I believe them?
—C.S. Lewis, *A Grief Observed*

Stepping out of the shower, he quickly dried himself off before tossing the towel aside. He picked up the soft white cotton bathrobe and pulled it on over his shoulders. He pulled the matching white fabric belt tight around his waist and tied a knot in the front. He then walked out of the bathroom and exited the building into the warm afternoon sun. It was a normal spring day. The sun was shining brightly overhead among billowy clouds floating across the canvas of a cerulean sky.

His eyes searched across the field of green grass, scanning each pass-erby for her. The college campus was teaming with students of all ages, walking and talking in pairs and groups, some alone, lost in their own thoughts. Some people moved quicker than others did, weaving through the slower groups of humanity.

He quickly spotted her, standing a short distance away with her back to him. She was wearing a similar white bathrobe as the one he wore. Her tanned legs extended beneath the hem where her tanned bare feet met the soft grass. As he walked toward her, it did not strike him as odd that they were both wearing white bathrobes in the middle of the day outside. Her long dark-brown hair hung down, cascading over her shoulders in sharp contrast to the intense snow white of the bathrobe.

As he came close, something told him to slow his pace, and he stopped and stared. She tossed her head, her hair flowing outward like a silky wave on the water. He could see by her movements that she was talking but could not hear her voice. She appeared to be having a conversation with an old man who he did not recognize. The old man sat directly in front of her in an old well-worn lawn chair. The distance between her and the old man appeared to be about two yards. The old man's eyes never wavered as he stared hard straight at her, the wrinkles of his skin extending outward from the corners of his eyes, his thin lips turned up in a foul grin. The old man stared, never taking his eyes off her, oblivious to the movement around him, listening intently to the words she spoke.

Suddenly, without his thinking, his legs began to move. As if drawn by an invisible string, he found himself walking toward her and this stranger who sat in front of her. His paced quickened, and he covered the distance quickly. This all seemed wrong, so wrong. His instincts raised the hairs on the back of his neck as he began to run.

The area around him was crowded with people milling about amid numerous large brick buildings, although he paid it no mind. He weaved his way through the throng as quickly as he could, his eyes never leaving her. He did not notice the coolness of the grass as it changed to dry and rough weeds under his bare feet.

As he drew closer in his approach to the two figures, he heard the sound of her voice softly on the wind. He came down to a jog, breathing hard. His confusion swirled as his heart beat loudly in his chest. She seemed to be replying in response to a question from the strange old man that he had not heard. Others continued to pass by ignoring them, all lost in their own worlds, even though the trio was oddly out of place, two dressed only in white bathrobes and an old man seated in a lawn chair in the middle of the grassy field between the large brick buildings.

Coming up from behind, she was unaware of his approach. His bare feet made no sound, and his nearness allowed him to hear her clearly say the word cancer. *He felt time stop in that moment as the word hung in the air. His legs suddenly felt heavy; everything around him moved in slow motion.*

He saw her hands come up out of the pockets of the robe and reach in front of her. He saw the ends of the white fabric belt fall to hang at her sides. He watched in fascination as she bent her arms at the elbow, her hands not visible to him as she held them in front of her. Suddenly, her arms flew out from her sides, tearing open her robe. Her hands held the edges of the robe; arms extended, the robe stretched like wings. In his mind, he could see the view of her from the front as her body stood still in the figure of a cross with both arms extended outward from her sides.

Shocked, his mind whirled, and the ground swayed as he struggled to maintain his balance. Time suddenly resumed its normal pace, and he shook the unsteadiness from his mind and quickly covered the last few yards to where she was standing. Without hesitating, he flung himself squarely between her and the old man sitting in the lawn chair. His back to her, he glared at the old man and saw the deliriously evil grin on his face. His crooked teeth showed yellow behind the thin pale lips. He stood staring at the old man who sat unmoving and indifferent to his presence other than leaning slightly to the side in an attempt to look around him. He moved in rhythm with the old man to block his view of her with his own body.

This quiet dance went on for several seconds when his mind suddenly registered a moment of clarity. As he had moved to intersect the sight line between her and the old man, he recalled he had been even more surprised to catch sight of bare skin and the swell of her breast. The realization that she was completely naked beneath the bathrobe and had exposed herself to this strange man sent his mind into a free fall as his knees buckled.

Catching himself before he fell, he took a deep breath to steady his mind. The dizziness had returned as he turned quickly, grabbed the edges of her robe, ripping them from her hands, and pulled them together to cover her nakedness. She did not resist, her arms falling to her sides. With shaking hands, he tied the waist strap in a knot to hide her nakedness, never looking into her eyes. He then grabbed her by the shoulders and spun her quickly away from the stranger. She acquiesced easily without complaint to his leading, and they began walking away as he guided her with his arm around her shoulders. Others continued to pass by, none seemed to have noticed the display, and for that, he was grateful.

As they walked, his legs felt unsteady and weak as if he had just ran a marathon. His mind told him they must get away, and he only kept moving on instinct. His mind was reeling; his heart again beating loudly in his chest. He wondered if the old man was following them, but he dared not look back. Minutes passed as they walked in silence, the world around them melting away, before he was finally able to speak.

"What are you doing?" he asked incredulously trying to hide the anger and shock as he turned his face toward her.

She would not look at him and stared straight ahead. Her response was short and terse with very little emotion. "You do not understand."

"I do not understand?" he questioned her, fighting to quell his surprise and rage that was growing.

"No, you do not," she stated simply, still not looking at him as they continued to walk.

The words hung in the air as she paused before taking a breath. He watched her as she continued to look straight ahead, staring off into the distance as she calmly added in a tone of finality, "I am the one dying."

The words she spoke pierced his heart, the pain shooting through him, and his world went black.

Deciphering Dreams

This is one of the few dreams I have had about Luka in all the years since her death. Yes, she is the girl in the white bathrobe, and I am the man in the matching white bathrobe. I woke from this dream in a state of frenzy as you might imagine from the graphic detail of revealing herself to a stranger. The mind has a will of its own. Some define dreams as simply a serious of images, ideas, or emotions that occur involuntarily in the mind during certain stages of sleep. Is there a larger interpretation or reason for this dream? I really do not know.

I have puzzled over the meaning and, still to this day, view this dream as an interesting parable, if you will, that the roads we travel are ours and ours alone. Her comment to me that I did not understand as she was the one dying speaks of truth. Although we can walk side by side sharing the experiences, ultimately, we cannot share everything. Our experiences are ours alone, and in the end, every couple, every individual must venture alone into the alone.

When we uttered the words until death do us part, we never expected that we would be facing the reality so soon. I am not sure if it would be different after forty, fifty, or sixty years instead of five as that was not my experience. There was no screaming remorse for the things not done and asking for forgiveness for promises not kept. There was no screaming at and into the darkness about the inevitable end we all must face or the unfairness of this life, for fairness is often not the point. Life just is, as is death.

The nights were the worst when the world is quiet. That is when my thoughts could run amuck. There was no relief from the mind that keeps turning, and time seems to slow to a crawl. The space before dawn seems so far away, and nothing will hasten it. I just do not know why. The memories still clamor for attention, asking what if this and that. There is regret that still lingers. In those moments, the voices scream the loudest and haunt the broken heart.

We tell ourselves we were not enough, especially as men. If only we had done something different or better, the outcome would have been different. The mind, when free from the trappings of reality, wanders where it will, making fantasy and magic a concrete thing. If only I could have known, this story—my story—would have been so much different.

After the first diagnosis, maybe even before that, because of her illness as a child. we were traveling on different roads. She had long ago turned off the road that I travelled. Oh, they would intersect at times, or the paths would parallel each other, but she was the one dying on a much faster schedule than I was, and still I find myself held too.

"I am the one dying."

The phrase is haunting, and she never said the words to me while alive. It was only after her death in a dream. I recall now how during her dying, she often seemed to be finding ways to ease out of life, softening the bonds and the ties to the things she loved of this world. There was nothing but subtle easy gestures where the distance between us seemed to grow. The veil seemed thinner; she glimpsed her leaving, while I railed against it, unwilling to face the truth. In the end, she stopped looking to me and began to look through me. She loved me, of this I have no doubt, but again, she was the one leaving, the one dying.

I have read the comment that it is an uncommon understanding of love, this love that glimpses its end. Luka's love for me allowed her to let go. She loved her life, believed in better things ahead, and obeyed its way of ending. I failed her in that I did not understand the enormous labor that dying required of her, not just dealing with the relentless physical pains and discomfort, but she also had to deal with my unwillingness to face the truth that was in front of me. I did not have any sense of grace about her dying and a belief that life, my life and her life, were simply going as they must.

Whatever side of dying we find ourselves on, we must be willing to see things for what they are and what they ask of us. With hope, courage, and faith, we stumble forward through lives filled with ambiguity until we are staring at the end.

Do we willingly acknowledge the truth that disease will do to us what it does faithfully or otherwise? Moreover, do we faithfully or otherwise go along with it? Our lives here on this earth, all life, will end in death for we are all dying, and when it happens, we find it to be such surprising news.

CHAPTER 8

The Lingering Ambiguity

*Ambiguity: the quality or state of being
ambiguous especially in meaning.*
—Merriam-Webster Dictionary (online version)

The online *Merriam-Webster* dictionary further defines ambiguity as "a word or expression that can be understood in two or more possible ways: an ambiguous word or expression." In addition, they define ambiguous as "doubtful or uncertain especially from obscurity or indistinctness" or "capable of being understood in two or more possible senses or ways."

Many questions linger still, memories that leave me confused to this day. Many moments have multiple possible interpretations, some I have interpreted in a certain way and believed as truth.

Other times, my fears get in the way. I find that often, we can be more fearful of others knowing we are afraid, more than what we are actually afraid of. Is not that what death, grief, pain, and even life can do to us all?

I think back to the afternoon when Luka was dying, the emotions that swirled about that small hospital room in the last moments of her life. It ran the extremes of loud visceral pleading to quiet shepherding while Luka lay still, silently voicing her choice of enough already. The skills required to love someone who was leaving was sorely lacking in the room that day.

The initial shock and reality of Luka's death created feelings of craziness within me. Moreover, grief can lead people to do crazy things but that doesn't mean the person is crazy. These feelings lead to disagreements, disappointments, conflict, and confusion that erupted over the ensuing days.

Wading through the legal and societal logistics of death is overwhelming, especially when your mind is anywhere but in the present. As her spouse with power of attorney, I scratched my signature with a shaking hand on the hospital paperwork in the hours following Luka's death.

I recall her mother, who had come to town the previous week, requesting that Luka's body remain in the hospital room. Luka's dad was flying in from Florida later that night, and she wanted him to be able to say goodbye. Standing in the hallway in front of the nurses' station, my nerves frayed, I responded in anger.

"No, I do not want her lying dead in that damn hospital bed for hours. He can see her at the funeral."

She said something about him needing to say goodbye. My empathy was nonexistent as thoughts of why he was not here already as his daughter had been dying swirled in my head. Often during her illness, I had held Luka as she cried over the longing that her parents were so far away.

I turned to her and I stated bluntly before walking away, "Well if he really cared, he would have been here before his daughter died."

I found out the next day, after I had left the hospital, Luka's mother had coerced the staff to leave her lying there for hours until her father arrived later that evening. I was extremely upset at her parents and the hospital staff. I felt like I was losing control of everything. First Luka dies, and now no one is listening to me. My world was spinning completely out of control. The world kept telling me I was not good enough. I could not protect her in life, and now I could not protect her in death.

Death brings out the best in people and the worst. There are things I said and regret, and there are things others said and did that infuriated and confused me. Her parents did not show up for the meeting with the pastor to discuss funeral arrangements. Her mother had to go buy a dress or get her hair done with a friend or something is what I remember hearing. I was angry that they failed to show and left all the arrangements and decisions to me. However, in hindsight, that may have been for the best as the people that were there did support me, and I probably would not have let them make any decisions anyway.

Our funds were low, with Luka in school and my meager salary at the time. Most of our money had been paying for the ongoing medical expenses. When Luka died, I had no idea the financial cost that was involved in death. My grandfather stepped in and paid for the funeral home costs. There was a plethora of plants and flowers provided free of charge by some friends who owned a local shop. Their children attended the day care where Luka had worked for years. They provided everything free of charge for the service at the church. I was living in a world of ambiguity surrounded by miracles, and nothing made any sense.

A Vague Sense of Wrongness

The demeanor of Luka's parents continued to confuse me. I knew they were hurting, but they seemed so aloof and so distant, and I was lost inside my own fog of overwhelming loss. I struggled with that; they were family after all and a last connection to Luka. I carried a lot of anger inside, wondering what they were feeling and thinking.

A week after her death and a few days after the funeral, I stood with her parents in the driveway of the house Luka and I shared, saying our goodbyes. I do not recall the actual words, but her father made a comment about how I would be okay because I would find somebody else. I remember just looking at him, unable to respond. The words exploded in my head as the ground swelled under my feet, and my mind screamed, *Are you kidding me! Really! Really! I will find somebody else. Your daughter, your only daughter just died, and now you stand here telling me I will find someone else? Just a week after her death!*

My mind was blown! This comment really floored me, and I still do not know what to do with it. I remember I did not react; I just remained stoic while raging and exploding inside. I probably showed a strained smile; it was never easy with him. I think he was well-intentioned, but the comment in that moment rang so hollow and untrue.

Luka's parents left town and went back home to Florida. Luka's brother went back home with his family, and I have never spoken to him, nor seen him since he left Boise in April of 1993. Luka's mother would call every couple of weeks to "check in" on me, but the conversations always seemed strained, and we only talked about surface things. It seemed neither of us could connect with the other. I did not know what she wanted or wanted to hear, and I did not want to share anything with her. I wanted the pain to myself.

The calls became more infrequent as the months went by. They came to town later that fall for a funeral. We spoke briefly while they were there, and they left without saying goodbye as I remember, and that was the last time I spoke to either of them. The end of a life changes many things, including relationships and families as they once were. The whole affair still carries a vague sense of wrongness in my mind. When hearts are broken, dreams are shattered, and it tears apart your world. Who can say what is right or wrong?

Free Falling

My world, my life, continued in a free fall after Luka's death. I tried to hide and to get on with life, my life. The reality of life and death had risen up from that place where our primal fears reside and smacked me full in the face. I was unprepared for this reality, refusing to accept it for the longest time.

This is not the normal order of things, I reasoned. We fall in love, get married, live our lives, have children, and welcome grandchildren into our families as we grow older together until we reach the end where one or the other of us has to venture alone into the undiscovered. Isn't that how it is supposed to work? That is what they told me; I am sure of it. Dazed and confused, I struggled forward, mindless to any type of future, only wanting to return to the past.

Over time, others have drifted away, even some family and friends, content not to witness my pain and the sadness in my eyes I believed. I have spent tremendous amounts of effort to hide my sorrow. I became an expert at pretending that I was okay while living in the endless days and nights of vague nothingness. They all resumed their safe little lives, spinning their safe little stories, and ignoring the reality, the reality we all have to face one day, or so I told myself.

The death of loved ones and our own haunts our waking and sleeping in this life. When death finds us, we should not stay there to wallow in self-pity for too long. I would spend hours sitting in the desert that summer, watching the sunset and thinking of Luka. It was always quiet and peaceful way out there, away from the clamor of others and the reality that lay in front of me. I sat alone, left with a life on my own with so many promises unfulfilled.

My mind would wander and remember that it was here, that this is where it all started. Luka and me in the desert, "us" together, we believed we could tackle the world. Then the world hit back. We walked through our own hell together, until life tore us apart.

Sometimes we do what we think we need to do, and then later, we wonder why we did that. I sat alone in the desert, rereading the letters we wrote to each other when Luka was a nanny in Dallas before we were married. I rationalized this as I was already in pain, so torturing myself further was no big deal. Those letters written years before when we were dating spoke of my feelings now, even though now, the finality of it all was I knew she was now never coming back.

> I feel like my inspiration is gone.
> I'd do it the same way and fall for you again if I
> had the chance.
> Part of me is missing.
> It's not just you and me but—us!
> The future's scary, isn't it? It's not gonna be easy.
> I have a feeling.

We never know how tough life will be, or at least, we are often unwilling to acknowledge it, but on some level, do we? Despite all the pain, heartache, sorrow, and sadness, everything else was worth it all to hold the memories of love.

Seeking Meaning

The night is getting too dark to read or write. The desert is quiet, and the sunset was good. Too many low clouds on the horizon blocked a lot of the light though. I find solace in the darkness of the night; almost a full moon is blazing as it climbs its way up from the underworld depths.

Suddenly, I am ranting and raving, and it is almost completely dark except for the bright light of the full moon. It just silently hangs in the dark sky, not caring about my pain. My anger burns hot and bright in the darkness. I tasted the salty sting of tears as they roll down my checks and over my lips. "God, I hate crying, but I thank you that I am alone here in the desert." I scream into the darkness at the moon in the eastern sky. The moon hangs in silence absorbing my anger.

"Here I am again, alone in the dark. God, I wish I could see you again, ya know. I mean a vision or something, just something so I would know you are okay. I want to believe that you are, at least I think I believe it, that you are happy. I will be too, and that is okay. Is that too much to ask? I mean, after all of this and what I have been through, the pain, the longing, the ache that never goes away?"

I turn to look to the ever-darkening western sky as the sun has sunk below the horizon. A dark bank of high clouds stretches upward from where the earth meets the sky. The darkness seeps into my heart, and the clouds suffocate my hope. Suddenly, enormous lightning strikes flash once, twice, three times. Seconds tick by as distant thunder rolls. I watch the sky as silence settles, until several smaller strikes occur with longer intervals in between.

"Is that a sign from God? Maybe saying, 'It is okay, I'm in control. See, I can make the heavens light up.'" The thoughts run through my mind as I sit shaking, my mind reeling.

Was this merely a coincidence? I have pondered this event often since then. Lightning is always awesome and beautiful no matter where you are. I had been staring in silence to the east at an almost full moon as it rose in the dark sky. What made me turn to the west and the setting sun? Could it be divine guidance or inspiration such that the human mind cannot define?

The days passed as I tried to make sense of the event, seeking some meaning, and I was still alone in my dark nights of ambiguity. I found myself left alone in the dark, even in the bright light of day. Occasional condolences still rolled in, but the wound was still too fresh and raw; true healing was still a long ways off.

We must believe in hope when our faith is as small as a wisp of smoke, a single light far off in the dark, that is all, a small thing that keeps me going before my hearts stops beating, while I keep hearing the banging sounds of drums repeating, for faith is the hope of things unseen.

Events happen throughout our lives; hard times come with often no meaning and no end in sight. Loved ones die, and there is no response from beyond the veil, only silence, as the undiscovered beckons to each of us silently with an eternal hope beyond this life, with no confirmation of what may actually come. Do we silently maintain faith with an expectation of the glorious promises of what may come? We can, and should, hold hope for others and ourselves in those dark times of ambiguity.

I was still stumbling forward, reconciling Luka's death and my own pain, as my grief lingered, as my life began to stir toward itself. I was just beginning to learn how to embrace my life as it was now, not as I wished it to be, for that was the only way to see a future. The grief in my heart I must carry, allowing it to occupy a place where I could accept the truth that she was gone and yet, someday—yes, someday…

Part 2

EMBRACING THE PRESENT

CHAPTER 9

Wearing Masks—"Who Are We Really?"

What hides behind the smiles and the vacant
eyes? Aren't we tired of wearing masks?
—Mark Wayne

Years later, as I reread my journals written in the months after Luka's death, there are many entries written in my shaking hand that mention my tiredness at pretending, faking it that I was okay, that I am strong. I hid so others would not see my pain. Looking back, I pretended a lot after she died and for many years thereafter. It is just now that I am seeking authenticity to be who I believe God created me to be; thus, this book is a small result of that.

We stare into the mirror and often wonder who that is behind those eyes staring back at us. There behind the masks we wear, living inside, we know and see those mysterious eyes of an imposter. Each day there is a fight that rages for us to be the person God created us to be. The war thunders continuously in our brains to be authentically real despite the constant fear and doubts, if only we were to believe the truth of who we are.

How often do we hide, camouflaged if you will, from others and even ourselves? The false image we present to the world can eventually become our reality, and then it colors everything we know and are. This is not truth but a lie. We will only find freedom in healing the broken places deep inside we all carry. Therein lays the paradox we wrestle, for the struggle is real, reckoning who we are, who we wish to be, and who we were created to be.

I find myself in an endless maze running from the darkness, seeking the light that is always just out of reach, chasing a dream that fades from my sight. I am a soul lost in the beauty of the eternal all around me as I search, seeking answers in the depths of my infernal sorrow. Others only see the smiling mask I wear for I never let them see behind the veil, for inside the violence quakes, and I live immersed in my own self-doubt and hate. This is the paradox of me.

Trapdoors fill my life's journey. I struggle forward, dancing in a minefield of shame. It seeks to steal my peace and joy, its only mission to inflict pain. I dance on, believing in the price that must be paid when the voices of regret scream in a never-ending rain. I wrestle with the demons that taunt me into believing that I need and must do a little bit more. This is the paradox of me.

Awake late in the night, I count the cost of a single soul, wayward and lost. In the morning's early light, I wake in dread of the names written on the eternal scroll, a smile I still carry on my face while my anxiety rages as I read my life's story written on the yellowed pages. My long-lost hope feels cold as I believe I am forgotten and alone. Yet in a single heartbeat, I rest in the grace and this small flicker of belief that I still hold. This is the paradox of me.

The Questions

What is your truth?

What is the truth you chose to believe?

How do you see yourself? How do you believe others see you?

Will you drop the camouflage and emerge, or will you continue to hide?

Are you more than what you allow others to see?

Could you be more than the mask you wear?

Who are you really?

We struggle between the eternities as we reckon with who we believe we are, who we wish to be, and who God created us to be. Ephesians talks about us being a masterpiece of his artisanship, if only we could believe how might the world and we be different, better.

We hide inside, forcing smiles and veiled laughter at the absurdities of life, shrugging off the pain as if it were of no more importance than…the inconvenience of a mosquito.

I spent so many years hiding, my heart in tatters, bruised and broken, that I let no one see. For, you see, I would not even go there. Why? What for? She died, and she is dead, I reasoned. *What is the use?* I would think to myself. All the while, my mind, heart, and soul are silently screaming I want more, while the enemy whispered in my ear, "Are you sure you can handle more?"

A simple little question, and the seeds of doubt would sprout to grow into towering evergreens, seemingly indestructible right where the enemy dropped those seeds. I plodded through my days, often feigning a reluctant acceptance because, you know, cowboys don't cry; they just ride away.

"I'm fine."

"Yeah, I am good."

"No worries"

"No, I don't need anything."

For behind the mask I stood stoic, not allowing anyone to see the real me and the hurt and pain inside that I hid. Hands of cruelty, others' laughter I interpreted as their own enjoyment of my misery, a misery they could not even see. It squeezed my heart until it burst apart. Stolen from my lungs was my truth, yanked out of my mouth while I uttered no sound, and my reality became an abstraction of days and nights of ambiguity. I was an unknown imposter to others, silently hiding undercover, even from myself, and no one knew.

> *I am singularly who you want me to be behind this mask, which is all I show.*
> *My life is carefully constructed behind this mask; life is a stage upon which I play.*

Only being who you want me to be behind this mask, I silently scream and stay.

Struggling with doubts that it will end, and a day of reckoning will dawn.

When eternity seeks me, and I will find, I gave my life to be the devil's ugly pawn.

A hope still lives that much more is offered, to be real in truth by the one who is all love.

Turning my back on the promises, He has silently wept while watching from above.

Is it too late to start anew, to emerge from the dark and find hope of renewed life?

To simply be real, casting aside the self-imposed chains of bondage that cause the strife.

The worldly deception is strong; it will never let go without a passionate fight.

For his grip on me and his will can only be broken by love's outrageous pure light.

My prayer to have him banished from the depths, from the dark places in my heart.

Shining through the cracks is a holy light, to shed this mask seems the best place to start.

I will fight the demons, this alien charlatan who lies and whose will is to rule.

I will stand firm and unafraid, I will no longer be just an unwitting fool.

To live my life as who I was meant to be, to be authentic and real.

Loving him with heart, soul, and mind, and to love others as myself is the deal.

When I discard this mask, there is a destiny and a mission, a path that is cleared for me.

I will rise on wings like a phoenix from the ashes, for I know now the impostor lies.

And the one who hides behind this mask is not me.

Then there is this, an effort to capture a truth I so desperately want to believe in.

> *My name is Mark Wayne Schutter,*
> *son and prince of the one true God,*
> *loyal servant to the true King, Jesus Christ.*
> *Husband to a beautiful wife,*
> *father to an amazing daughter;*
> *and I will stand against evil*
> *in this life and the next!*

I wrote the words above in December of 2004 based on a scene from the movie *Gladiator*. In the scene, Maximus turns to face the emperor, Commodus, when asked what his name is. This was one month after my daughter was born and eleven and one-half years after Luka's death. I often find myself still wondering to this very day who I am and often in need of a reminder. Our lives are so much more than what we see, for there is eternity placed in our hearts. Words of truth so easily stolen vanish into the darkness like smoke into the night. Yet one small light can carve the dark and cast out the doubts. We must see that the light does not go out. How would you, how do you answer when asked for your name?

Future Opportunities?

The doctor was silent as he quickly stitched skin taken from my thigh, grafting it to the back of my left hand. After finishing the bandaging and giving me instructions on care and cleaning, this very nice doctor who did not know me other than as a patient began to tell me how lucky I was and the many opportunities that lay before me for my future once I walked out of his office. He was referring not to my hand or head and the healing of the many physical wounds but of my recent loss and Luka dying. It had come up during the intake and admittance to the hospital after the car accident, so he knew my recent history that had led to me landing in his office as a patient.

Walking out into the July sunshine, I did not think that I had any future, and the doctor's words rang hollow. I only felt more of the same, more pain, darkness, hurt, and regret, just trying to get through the rest of July and August to deal with the upcoming anniversaries of firsts. This train was not stopping, I wanted off as I sat in the back seat of my parents' car on the drive back to Boise, clutching a proverbial suitcase in my lap that contained nothing. There was nothing that I could bring along on this wretched journey that would do me any good.

I prayed to God night after night to take me while I slept and that I would not awake. I would lie awake, picturing the major events of the past few years, all of which led to the very real possibility that the car accident may have been an unconscious attempt to kill myself.

I was unsure without Luka in my life, and all I could see was more emptiness. Everything was a reminder of all she had left behind. A part of me lived day by day in dreaming that somehow I would no longer be part of this world.

I think about all the prayers said speeding them on to heaven and never getting an answer to those prayers. What is a person, especially a man, supposed to do with the thought that he could not save her? I did what I thought I was supposed to do most of the time. I was the dutiful son, the responsible one, the one who could and would survive. Do not let anyone down, and especially, do not disappoint them. This was my cross of truth I was to carry, I believed.

Although I tried, I could not save her or myself. At least the darkness covered the bleeding like a heavy blanket. Some say God has a purpose for what we strive for and what we want, and his plan is to perfect us in the pain. It is hard for me to wrap my head around that as I do not believe God's design or plan was to take out of this world a bright young woman who had so much to offer, who was truly a gift to me. She taught me so much and molded me into becoming a better man. Can I get to a point where I believe in the goodness of a God who would take one of his children to teach another one a lesson?

I do not believe in a god that would willingly separate happy people only to give them something better. She was not a thing, an inanimate object; she was a living, breathing human being, a child of God who loved him, others, and me.

I still wonder at the seeming randomness of this as I have no idea why any of this happened. There was no drunken driver, there was no intruder in the home, no secondhand smoke, nothing like that that I can blame, that I could point to, just this sickness of cancer. It grew inside her body, mostly unseen, where it thrived and grew invisible beneath her skin.

A sharp pain in a mundane moment of life and the blood work, X-rays, and invasive medical procedures revealed this hideous thing inside. Cancer—just the word changes everything, and oh my god, how it all affected her emotionally and physically would fill up another book. Eventually, it took her life, and I could not figure out how to stop it. It affected our lives; how could it not? The pain that assailed her I could do very little about, so I wandered, feeling helpless. Helplessness is not a feeling men deal with very well.

My dilemma even now to this day and the actual question is, was there something that I missed? Our culture raises boys to be strong and to protect those who are vulnerable, especially our family. That is what the wedding vows say, to love and protect, to honor and cherish in sickness and health. I tried, I tried my best, and it seems it still was not enough.

We travel the roads of this life saying hello and saying goodbye to those we meet, come to love, and let go. Men go forward and rarely allow others to see beyond the masks we wear, and we live with our supposed failures.

We are all broken, and if we can come together, sometimes those broken pieces of you and me will come together beautifully. That is something I am just now learning. The shared human experiences are what bring us together, the ability to, every once in a while, remove the mask and emerge from the behind the facade to face the doubts that still linger.

Are you wearing a mask?

If so, ask yourself why and seek healing

Will you remove your mask if you are asked to?

CHAPTER 10

A Different Trajectory

Where there is sorrow, there is holy ground.
—Oscar Wilde

I did not understand or accept it then, but I understand and accept it now...or at least, I understand and accept it a little more. I tell myself this as I carry the questions into the future, and it serves as a small comfort to my tired soul.

I am sitting in a coffee shop on a Wednesday on an early November night with my wife while our daughter is at AWANA's. We come here at the same time each week where we have a couple of hours of time together, just the two of us. My laptop is open to an early draft of this book, papers and journals spread around me on the table as I contemplate what to write. The sounds of a low hum of human interaction and silence are a perfect combination around me. I feel the warm and safe embrace in sharp contrast to the rain and darkness outside as I stare out the window next to me. This chapter has me stumped. I brought along an old journal, and I began leafing through papers tucked inside.

I remove a pile of lined sheets of green paper. Pull out a stack of five-by-eight-inch spiral-bound pages folded in half. Opening up the pages, I begin reading the words on the first page. In the upper left corner, in all capital letters in my own handwriting is the date, Wednesday, February 6, 1991, and the first sentence.

Here it is, February already. I just can't believe it.

I read on while the memories began to swirl as I recalled that I wrote these lines still two years before Luka died. As the normalcy of a Wednesday evening at the coffee shop continues around me, patrons sip drinks, some chatting with friends, others reading or writing, headphones blocking out the world around them.

I slowly sip my black coffee and continue reading my own writings about a journey that started eight months before in June of 1990, recounting the blur of hospitals, doctors, nurses, medicines, and insurance claims, all the while continuing to work and carry on life as usual to the best of our abilities. It strikes me as surreal to realize the writing is my own, and the story is my life.

Then I read that I was trying to put up a good face while responding to inquiring minds.

Yeah, I'm fine, and everything
is going to be all right.

The words stopped me in my tracks as my eyes filled with tears. I am fine. Everything is going to be all right. Lies, lies I told others and myself in an effort to deny the reality.

That pain and hurt is part of life, and there are things you never return from, at least not completely. We often end up going in a different direction than was planned, like a river overflowing its banks during a flood creating new paths. We are at the mercy of the river, sometimes caught in its swift current. Things happen, and we must just continue to paddle through the rapids of our lives. Often we know not where we are going, but sometimes, can we take comfort that it is enough to be going somewhere?

Class 4 Rapids

Luka physically hurt, her head pounding, and she could only sleep in short spells, which meant I could not and would not sleep. Just as the sky was beginning to lighten, I called the doctor's answering service before half carrying, half dragging her to the car. The pain in her head and hip seemed to worsen with each troubled step we took. She cried out in pain as she bent over, exclaiming in a terrified voice, "I feel like I am going to throw up."

The nausea had become a constant companion and seemed almost normal at this point. I had watched my beautiful wife vomit while holding her on so many occasions that it barely fazed me now. Upon finally getting her settled into the car, we rushed through the early morning downtown traffic to the Mountain States Cancer Institute (MSTI), known affectionately as Misty to those lucky and unlucky enough to have an occasion to walk through the doors.

After parking the car, I quickly went through the familiar sliding glass doors of this building we had visited so many times for chemotherapy, radiation treatments, tests, and oncology doctor visits. Despite the reason we were there, I moved with a steady confidence which masked my anxiety. I knew what I was doing and grabbed one of the wheelchairs just inside the doors.

Several minutes later the doors automatically opened again in front of us, and I pushed the wheelchair through with Luka in it, her head slumped forward toward her chest. Her hair hung down over her shoulders obscuring her face, but I could hear her quiet moans and deep breaths. I knew deep down this was not good, and my heart was racing, beating loudly in my chest. Out of the corner of my eyes, I saw the many patients already in the waiting area even at this early hour. I checked her in with the receptionist at the front desk, and we sat down to wait.

My heart beat loudly in my chest, and my anxiety spiked. I glanced around the room nervously. Sitting in the plastic leather-covered chair with Luka barely coherent beside me in the wheelchair, I hid in plain sight from everyone in the room. I suddenly realized that she was going to vomit again.

I had developed an anticipatory instinct, noticing the slightest change in her that signaled the inevitability. Her chest convulsed with a huge breath, and her Adam's apple bobbed up and down slightly as her dry lips parted repeatedly. Her breathing began coming in shallow gasps, and I yelled at those behind the counter that I needed a garbage can or something.

The receptionist appeared not be fully awake and ignored my pleas. The room of patients and caregivers went silent; I was moving in a silent picture show, all sound around me now shut off. People stared, but I saw nothing but Luka in front of me. I looked quickly up to the counter and the small group of receptionists and nurses behind the counter stared at us. Again I yelled into the silence of the room as my anger and trepidation grew, "She is going to throw up! Doesn't anybody here give a shit?"

My voice reverberated loudly against the walls, shaking one of the staff out of her early-morning sleepy trance. She moved quickly, and I watched her ponytail swishing back and forth behind her head as she came toward us. With a timid hesitant look on her face, she handed me a small plastic wastebasket. I snatched it from her hands, thrusting it under Luka's chin and mouth just as she vomited hot bile into the can.

The liquid spewed from Luka, making a splattering sound as it hit the plastic of the can as her retches filled the room. I heard gasps around me from others as the staff member backed away quickly. A nurse approached us and mumbled something about finding us a private room. I gave the nurse a hard look while my mind screamed, *Yeah, that's probably a good idea, stupid!*

I stood quickly, looking around the room at the wide-eyed people sitting silently and staring, many fighting their own battles. The confusion, shock, and even hints of compassion only served to fuel my anger. As my helplessness boiled over, I shouted over my shoulder as we left the waiting room, "What the f—— are you all staring at!"

You carry the pain, the hurt, the confusion with you, hidden deep inside. It appears to all who see that you are whole, complete. You carry an uncertainty because you know you are not the same.

The wound may heal, but the scars remain like tracks across your heart. Sometimes the scars are numb, sometimes raw and bleeding.

You move forward, hesitantly at first as the image you bear becomes easier, and it becomes who you are. Whether the image is the truth or a lie, the mask distorts the image into the reality. Streaks of light may illuminate the dark, casting shadows of memories of what might have been. We can find ourselves pulled toward the light and a hope that still burns. However faint, the glowing embers smolder, promising a new tomorrow, and sometimes we do not want that tomorrow. We want what has already passed.

Even now, I still struggle with this, although I am better than I used to be. I have wandered in ambiguity for so long, seemingly trapped between the physical and spiritual realms in this dark night of my soul. I did, and still do, rant about the injustice of meeting other's expectations that I tell myself are truth. I believe others expected me to pretend, so I did, and I hated others and myself for that. Caught in a culture that often espouses, the best thing you can do with death is to ride off from it.

Making a Choice

The light can grow and shine brightly if we let it. For brief moments, the light chases away the dark, chases away the fears. Living in the memories of another time is a false comfort with no hope for the future. To grab and hold the light blazing a new destiny is what we desire. To move, to love, to live, we must make a choice.

It is a brave, brilliant, courageous, and willing choice. I did not understand then, but I understand it now… I must continue to make that choice. We all must make that choice, for that one choice can be a stepping-stone, a stepping-stone when we fake it until we make it. We lie to others and even to ourselves.

"I am fine."
"She's in a better place."
"I am happy she is not suffering anymore."
"Thanks for stopping by."
"I appreciate your kind words."

"I am looking forward to next weekend."
"Thanks for inviting me."
While inside, I find myself silently screaming.
"Now get out."
"Leave me alone."
"I do not want to hear anymore."
"Are you serious?"
"That is all you've got."
"You do not understand."
"Do you really care?"
"Does anybody really care?"

Go back to your safe little life where you do not have to face the stark reality of an empty house, where ghosts do not wander the halls, and you hear her voice whispering in the wind through the trees every night, when the mere sight of a plastic hairbrush or a single shoe can stop you in your tracks, bringing you to your knees as gut-wrenching sobs pour forth from your body until you are empty with nothing left.

You fall into an exhausted sleep on the sofa instead of the bed because the bed is too empty, and she is not there. The silence is overwhelming, but if you strain hard enough, you can almost hear the sound of her breathing which used to gently lull you to sleep, but all that does is bring on another fit of crying, your face buried in the pillow as you curse God under your breath.

Will you stay with me then in those awful moments of anguish, and will you not turn away?

Behind the pain is the torment I have hidden, living inside the lies. I have held each lie close as my own crafted shield of truth. Those are but few of the lies I have told myself because really, I am fine.

Looking back, I wonder why, why the lies that insulated me? Why did I, and still do, lie to others and myself...in a word, fear, fear that drives us, motivates us, and often paralyzes us. We have all heard or seen the lists based on polls of the things people fear the most. These lists often include the following in no particular order: fear of flying, public speaking, spiders, snakes, dying, heights, pain, etc.,

etc., etc. We also have fears with social and emotional implications, rejection, disappointments, abandonment, ridicule, exclusion, etc., etc., etc.

I fear death, not my own but the death of those I love, of being alone and being helpless in the face of tragedy and watching someone you love live in pain. I wonder…

Somewhere, inside, on a deeper level, are we often more fearful of others simply knowing that we are afraid?

To allow our fear to be visible, well, this implies a transparency and vulnerability allowing others to see us truly as we are, to take off our masks that so easily become who we believe we are. Is it a matter of trust that others will not betray us when we are transparent and vulnerable? I know there are times when I often do not raise my hand, speak, or stand up when I should. I tell myself this is because I do not want to offend or to be a troublemaker. I label this fear as one of not wanting to be rejected, ridiculed, shunned, or even thought to be stupid. If God is not afraid of my questions, why should I be?

On an even deeper level, I now realize that it is true that *my overwhelming fear from which all others rise is simply this. It is a fear of others actually knowing that I am fearful.*

There are moments and events in each of our lives that leave us wondering and often searching for answers to questions that rattle in our minds. Yet even if we found those answers we so desperately seek, would they provide the comfort we seek?

We talk about grief as something that comes when tragedy and loss strike our safe little worlds we have created. We do not understand the purpose other than to view grief as an intrusion, something to understand and be done away with as quickly as possible, for the experience can and should irrevocably change us. How could it not? It is the natural order of things. We should seek what it is that grief asks of us.

I Wonder…

I believe that some questions very well remain unanswered this side of the undiscovered. C. S. Lewis in *A Grief Observed* talks about how in the midst of our pain we may ask nonsense questions that God finds unanswerable, and he simply waves them away in compassionate silence.

I am not saying here that our seeking and questions are nonsense; quite the opposite. They are our hearts' desire buried deep, calling out for truth in a world that is so often void of truth. On the other hand, we hear truth as told by others and their points of view to serve their own agendas.

I encourage you to continue to believe despite the silence. Does not faith believe in the unseen? Our hearts yearn for blessings of a grace that is beyond our wildest hopes. Remember that you matter, and there is a love and grace that changes people.

CHAPTER 11

Not Wanting to Be Alive

Not wanting to be alive is not the same
thing as wanting to be dead.
—Megan Devine, *It's Okay That You're Not Okay*

The world had crashed in on me and gotten much, much smaller. Since Luka's death, I did what I had to do, what I felt like I should do, and what others expected me to do, nothing else. It all came down to this; I was a widower at twenty-eight years old. The word seemed strange, made no sense as it rambled around in my head.

Just short of three months, the days and the world just rolled on one after another. The house was stale, empty, and I was still alone. There were things still that needed doing, especially feeding and caring for the dog and cats. Most other things did not seem to matter much. Whether my clothes are clean makes little difference to me, and the act of waking up each morning and getting out of bed and going to work was heroic enough.

I needed to get away. I felt it in every fiber of my being. I needed to break from the monotony of the painful days and the expectations of others. I had the idea to go to the coast to see the ocean. Luka loved the ocean. We had spent our honeymoon on the shores of the

Oregon coast, and now I felt drawn there. We had spent that week in the moment; our future and forever seemed so far away. We had the moment, we had that day, and for then, that was enough. I look back, and I see the mingling of our two lives and an uncertain future that neither of us could have predicted.

The thought of going back to the place where it all began now after our marriage had ended was scary, but it was as if some invisible tether was pulling me there. It was Friday, June 25 of 1993, and a very typical hot summer in southwestern Idaho with deep forever-blue skies overhead. The days were stifling hot even already in late June and the nights not much better, but that did not really matter; I did not sleep anyway.

Don't Close Your Eyes

The pull to go back to where it all began overrode my common sense. I was still sleeping on the futon in the living room with the dog and cats next to me. The bedroom still held too many painful reminders and the bed was too empty.

The coast beckoned as I backed the Ford Bronco II out of the driveway and left in the early morning after a long night of work. The Bronco was the first car we had purchased together, and now it was only mine. Next to me on the front seat was RC, our beloved little white mutt, a brown paper bag with an unopened bottle of brandy, my Bible, my harmonica, and some snacks. The Bronco hummed down the highway, and I had no other plans than to go to the coast. There was no place to stay when I got there. I was just headed out to get away on my own.

I drove into eastern Oregon with the sun rising steadily in the sky at my back. As I drove, I was fighting sleep and the urge to close my eyes. As I headed further west, the landscape turned from desolate desert into agricultural fields and back again. I felt like I was running from a thing that was chasing me, but I could not put it to words.

My eyes closed only for a second, and I jerked myself back awake, my heart pounding. RC was lying contently on the passenger seat, sleeping. I yawned and shook my head to wake myself. I spotted the sign alongside the road; only a few more miles up the road, and I will stop for a little break. I sped down the two-lane highway at 65 miles an hour, hoping these last few miles would go by quickly.

The Bronco drifted to the right, chewing up gravel as the passenger side tires drifted off the pavement. The vehicle started down the embankment. I suddenly woke with a start. I jerked and pulled hard on the steering wheel to the left, overcorrecting. The Bronco tires grabbed the asphalt, and the vehicle was suddenly airborne, flipping over and over down the road, and my world suddenly went black.

Visions of voices and arms around me intruded into my mind. I recognized the inside of an ambulance and a compassionate face looking down at me, forgotten words spoken, and then I found myself lying in a hospital bed with visions of Luka's dying body dancing through my head.

I stared at my left hand heavily bandaged in white gauze up to my forearm. I hurt all over, especially my head, and when I gingerly reached my right hand to my head, I felt the bandages wrapped around my head also. The pain medicine caused me to doze off again, and I awakened off and on throughout Friday night until Saturday morning.

I have no recollection of the doctors, nurses, or the medical procedures, including cleaning my wounds, picking the glass fragments out of my head and hand, nor the thirty-seven stiches they placed from just above my right eyebrow to the back of my head and everything else done to put me back together again. There were no broken bones, nor a concussion, but there were severe lacerations and bruises all over my body. Lucky to be alive, I was told. Truth, I did not feel lucky.

It appeared my left hand had smashed through the driver side window. The glass had shredded the backside of my hand to tatters. Several weeks later, in an outpatient surgery, they grafted skin taken from my upper right thigh to the back of my left hand. The graft closed the open wound all the way down to the bones. I carry those scars across the back of my hand from my knuckles down to my wrist as a reminder to this day.

Sometimes the scars we carry are angry, sometimes those scars scream, and sometimes those same scars still bleed, not in physical pain, although the spot on the back of my hand is still tender to hard pressure, and the scars turn an ugly purple color when my hands are cold. No, the emotions can still well up at unexpected moments, a quivering lip, tear-filled eyes, as a slow teardrop rolls silently down my cheek before I quickly wipe it away, hoping no one saw. Sometimes the scars whisper softly of a life and a love not forgotten, and sometimes looking at those scars is just what I need.

As I mentioned earlier in the book, whether I was unintentionally trying to kill myself, I do not know. Several days after leaving the hospital and back in Boise, I ventured to take a shower. Alone in the bathroom, I stared at the tired face staring back at me from the mirror. The eyes were sad, my head wrapped all in white. I slowly and gingerly cut through the tape, holding the gauze in place and, with trembling fingers, began to remove the bandages from my head.

As the three-inch gauze unwound from around my head, the end fell down until it began to pool on the floor. As the dressing that covered my head grew thinner, shades of pink and red from the wound began to show in splotches against the white gauze. The final swatches of cloth fell off, and I stood staring at someone I did not recognize. The right side of my head was shaved clean, and an ugly scar, a jagged red streak, ran from the middle of my forehead all the way to the back of my head, the skin on both sides of the bright-crimson line held together by thirty-seven dark stitches. I stood and stared, numb as no tears fell from my eyes, for I felt I had forgotten how to cry.

As I recuperated over the next couple of weeks, we pieced together stories of the accident in conversations. The last thing I remembered was waking to find the vehicle had drifted off the road. I overcorrected the steering, and everything went dark. Witnesses stated that when they approached the wrecked vehicle, they saw my shirt and pants covered in blood. After removing me from the wreckage, they also discovered my white socks were stained reddish pink from the blood that had dripped down into the cowboy boots I was wearing. Worst of all for me, RC, our beloved dog, was nowhere to be found.

My father and grandfather went back to the sight of the accident several days later. They even walked up and down the road looking for RC who they did not find. The Bronco's final resting place was an Oregon junkyard. They retrieved some of my personal belongings, including my dented harmonica, crushed during the accident, which I still have to this day.

I blame myself for making a bad decision. I blame myself for the accident. I blame myself for killing my dog. I have lived with each of these beliefs, bringing them into my present.

Over the next few weeks, I began to recover from my physical wounds, yet the pain in my heart was unrelenting. I sat in a chair at my parents' home, watching television or sleeping most days, oblivious to the world going on outside. The pain in my head and body was tolerable most days, thanks to the prescription pain pills.

One day, I found myself alone in the house. I awoke from sleep and noticed it was early afternoon. The television droned on. I had no idea what show was playing, and it did not matter. I had no idea how long I had been sleeping.

The pain in my head suddenly crashed through my consciousness, and the pounding was like the driving of nails into my skull. I still had the stitches in my scalp, and the wound was still raw and painful. I knew I had slept through a scheduled dose of pain medication and was now paying the price for it.

Sitting in the recliner, a blanket over my lap, I looked around and saw the prescription bottle on the kitchen counter. Knowing I had to get out of the chair, I pulled the blanket to the side and slowly rose from my seated position. As I stood up, the pain shot through my head, and I doubled over in agony. I steadied myself until the pounding subsided and was able to make my way to the kitchen counter in my stocking feet.

My hands reached for the edge of the counter, and I stood panting, the pain in my head throbbing. After several minutes, I reached for the pill bottle. I struggled to remove the childproof cap, my frustration and panic growing. The pain in my head pounded on unceasingly. When the cap finally came loose, the bottle spilled from my hand, sending pills scattering like drops of water skittering across the countertop. I grabbed one pill and quickly dry swallowed. I stood gripping the counter edge, my body shaking as the room spun around me. I waited, praying for the moment to pass.

I was so tired, so tired of the pain and the longing, and I felt the sheer exhaustion of it all wash over me. My mind was tired of the confusion, and my heart only wanted what I could not have, what I knew I could never have. I made a decision in that moment of pure torment.

Still I felt an urge not to leave the mess of pills scattered across the counter. With a shaking hand, I slowly I picked them up one by one and placed them back in the bottle. I struggled before finally replacing the little white cap as my world again went dark.

Some Things You Don't Come Back From

I found myself sitting in the office chair, my elbows resting on the dark wooden desktop. *How did I get here?* I thought. I had no recollection of getting there, nor even where I was exactly, but my mind was clear, clearer than I felt it had been in quite some time, and I knew what I wanted to do. I was so tired of not knowing what to do, and finally, in this moment, I felt as if I knew exactly what I wanted and needed to do.

I stared down at my bandaged left hand before slowly moving my eyes to the pistol that I clutched in my right hand. A box of shells was open on the desktop. Gently, I transferred the revolver to my injured left hand, and I cradled it gingerly. I slowly removed one bullet from the box, held it between my fingers, and stared. I slid the bullet into the empty cylinder before rolling it to the next empty chamber. I did this five more times until the cylinder was fully loaded. I closed the cylinder, the metallic click echoing in the silence.

I felt the coolness of the white pearl grip in my right hand, stark against the gunmetal gray of the pistol action and barrel. I stared at my father's pistol, one that I had shot many times before and that he

103

had promised would be mine one day. I felt no emotion, no remorse, no regret in that moment, only a cold and stony resolution. I had watched her die, and I could not save her, so now I would die.

I pulled back the hammer and brought the pistol up, pressing the round end of the barrel hard against my right temple. I tensed my index finger on the trigger. I felt abandoned and alone as I pressed my finger slightly tighter against the trigger. I felt the cold round metal of the barrel end making an indent into my skin. I was not sure I wanted to die, but I knew in those moments that I did not want to live anymore.

"I am sorry, Luka. I am sorry I let you down. I am so sorry for everything. Please forgive me."

Taking a deep breath, I prayed a silent prayer. Thoughts of shame, regret, and her flowed through my mind when I felt the hair on the back of my neck stand up. A cold wind swept over me, and I realized in that instant that my head was not hurting, only a dull almost nonexistent ache. I held the gun to my head, frozen, as the moments slowly ticked by in the silence of the room.

My mind cleared like strong wind blowing the fog from across the water. In a flash of surreal clarity, I realized I was in my parent's home. Then another thought ricocheted through my brain; they would find me.

"Oh, God," I stammered, still believing everyone would be better off without me, but something had stayed my hand. My own pain was almost too much and unbearable at times, and I would not wish that on anyone. Even in my state of despair and longing, my mind shifted. This was a burden I must carry. It was mine, and if that meant I was destined to carry it alone, then so be it.

I knew the loss would never go away, and no matter what I did to fill the empty spaces, her absence would always be permanent. This was no longer an option, and I had to move forward. I slowly lowered the pistol from my temple and quickly released the cylinder latch to eject all six shells. They clanged loudly in the silence as they hit and bounced across the wooden desktop. I snapped closed the metal cylinder of the now-empty revolver and laid it on the desk.

Methodically, I replaced each shell back in the box before slowly rising from the chair. Like a man much older than my twenty-eight years, the pain in my head had returned as I walked slowly out of the room on a hot July afternoon. I carry this memory with me, the finality of what might have been and what now would not.

I thank God for acts not committed and thought how that one act would have changed everything.

CHAPTER 12

Birthdays, Anniversaries, and Other Triggers

There are anniversaries we try hard to remember
And there are anniversaries we can never forget
—Mark Wayne

With tears behind my eyes, in the years since, I have often stood and stared at the endless expanse at the water's edge. Although my eyes were wide open, I would squeeze them tight so that no one can see, and nothing leaks out, for that would give away my feelings, and boys are not supposed to cry.

Yes, I realize I am hiding while surrounded in a frenzy of emotions that come and go until I am almost numb. Each "special" day—birthday, anniversary, and memory—as they come, rattles the things we hold dear, things we thought we long ago laid to rest.

I am angry! I am sad! I am frustrated and alone…

My stomach was in knots and my muscles tense as my mind reels. I feel the passion surging inside of me, like the unceasing waves of the ocean, and I am terrified of it spilling out into a fit of rage, while my mind spins with questions that have no answers, for I long ago learned there are none.

This is my story, my reality, and my life…

Each day rolled by in succession, the weeks, the months and the years, as if nothing has changed. Yet the birthdays, anniversaries, and triggers, the reminders that they are no longer with us, keep coming. We sometimes see them coming, and sometimes we do not.

Those dates on the calendar slowly approach. Some dates are clear as dancing flames of fire that burns a hole in the black. Those days can leave behind painful scars forever seared in our brain, memories of what was lost in the darkness of the past that slaps our hearts with regret.

She died from a cancer that invaded her body and mind, and yes, cancer sucks. Not a day goes by that something does not remind me of her. When she died, she left a hole in my heart. I watched the traditional treatments wreck and devastate her body, mind, and spirit. The health care system marched forward telling us we had no choice, for if you can, you should. You should fight this disease, this war and nothing less would be acceptable. Yet in the end, it did nothing to neither prolong her life, nor improve the quality of her life. So yes, I may still be jaded.

After she was gone, Luka's things still lay scattered all around the house, her hairbrushes, hair ties, perfumes, makeup, and her blow dryer on the side of the sink. Everything is exactly where she had left it, waiting for her return, and it struck me how it all seemed wrong. Everything was here, just as it was, and yet she was not and never would be again, and it was up to me to clean up the mess.

Birthdays

One month later following her death, the day of her birth into this world arrived, yet she was not there to celebrate. Each year, whether we celebrate or not, a birthday comes as a date on the calendar for each of us. There are birthdays that once were, some that are no more, and birthdays that still are. Every year Luka's birthday comes around again; this very day years ago, a small child was born. She was a life born into this world with a future yet unformed, just as we all were once. No one this side of the undiscovered knew the path this life would take, and no one knew how it would end.

Does it seem strange that after the death of someone we love, we often still remember and celebrate the day of their birth? When I say celebrate, I do not mean a party or anything of the sort as the day has taken on a completely new meaning. This is more of just a gentle reminder and an acknowledgment of the importance of this very day, for if we were to forget, would that be a sort of blasphemy?

Now that she was gone, this day is still the day of her birth when she came alive kicking and screaming into the world. On that day, specifically, I still pause and remember her fondly. The memory I hold so dear is nothing of how she would be now if she were to appear, for so many years later, she would have aged. She would carry more scars from the tragedy and heartache that life most certainly would have thrown at her.

Still I remember a young girl that I long ago wed when her birthday comes around each year on the same date. It reminds me of another lifetime and that she is still gone. Is it strange to mark the passing of the years, not by a new year each January 1 but by a seemingly inconsequential date on the calendar that most barely recognize?

So on the day of her birth each year, I acknowledge her. I convince myself I remember it all, or so I like to think. I have forgotten so much more than I will ever remember, but it seems that is okay today as I will never forget her. Each year on this day, I remember she would have been another year older. She would no longer be the young girl who captured my heart so many years ago but a middle-aged woman. I will leave that right here because I am not sure what to do with that.

Luka and I saw the movie *Highlander* for the first time at a midnight showing with friends a year before we were married. In the 1986 cult classic, there is a scene where the lead actor is at the bedside of his dying wife. She is dying of old age, looks up at him, and asks in a quiet voice for him to light a candle and remember her on her birthday. He looks at her with tears in his eyes and in a Scottish accent says, "Aye, love, I will."

After Luka died, starting with her first birthday just over a month after her death, I have lit a candle on that day as a reminder and acknowledgment of a girl who once lived. It is never a gaudy or over-the-top celebration, just a small token of remembrance that my life and who I am today was impacted by her, a small flame that signifies a life lived well to the very end.

It does not matter what color or type of candle. I have used whatever is handy in the moment over the years, no preplanning and no preparation. I do it on the day of her birthday, sometime during the twenty-four-hour period when the time feels right. The only requirement is a never-before-burned candle must be used. It is not the candle; the candle is only a vessel, for it is what the candle's flame signifies.

Striking a match head across the striker or a flick of the metallic lighter mechanism, the hot flame bursts forth, dancing in the air. The smell of sulfur wafts in the air as I stare at the flame for a moment before I slowly move the burning flame to the candle's wick. The flame licks the white string wick covered in wax. The flame dances around the wick that stands erect. It is seconds before it catches, and the wick ignites into its own flame.

The two flames mingle for a moment as one, dancing higher into the air, climbing, grasping one another, afraid to let go, intertwined now as one where before they were two and separate. Two beings become intertwined, their hearts beating as one after life has thrown them together. Now a single flame is dancing to the same unheard beat of the universe.

The hot yellow-orange flame mesmerizes me. It seems to speak to me of words spoken and promises kept. This small ritual has occurred every year on her birthday since her death.

Slowly I pull back my hand, and the one flame separates into two, just like two lives torn apart by forces unseen and beyond mortal control. The flame in my hand dies, while the candle flame continues to burn.

"I love you, Luka. Happy birthday." I whisper softly and utter a silent prayer for redemption before I turn away.

Good Friday and Easter

When they came to the place called The Skull, there they crucified Him and the criminals, one on the right and the other on the left. (Luke 23:33 NASB)

It was the third hour when they crucified Him. (Mark 15:25 NASB)

Frozen in time, eternal, etched in stone and in our minds, never forgotten, are some moments of our lives. Our memories burn hot of what is past. Every year as the stores begin to fill with decorations and supplies for the Easter holiday or resurrection Sunday, I cringe as it serves to remind me. She died on Good Friday, and now the Christian celebration of the crucifixion of Jesus Christ to save his followers from their sins reminds me of my own loss. I usually hide on this day, often seeking solace and solitude.

They crucified him, and as followers, we are to crucify our flesh and know him crucified. History tells us the crucifixion of Jesus took place at the third hour, approximately 3:00 p.m.; she died at approximately 4:00 p.m. Her flesh, her physical body, this disease crucified as she willingly allowed the crucifixion of her spirit with him and accepted him as the way, the truth, and the life, which is what I believe led to her being saved in the end.

On Sunday, the empty tomb and the resurrection of Jesus serve to remind the faithful of the hope we have. For me, that first Sunday after her death, Easter Sunday, I remember as a day of confusion, numbness, rage, and completing one expected task after another. Who knew death required so much from us at the time when we have the least to give.

Each succeeding Easter Sunday for so many years showed up as another day where the only resurrection are the memories that continue to rattle the chains in the attic of my mind. I wrote in my journal many years after her death:

> Another "special" day has come and went.
> No trumpets, no fanfare, and still no you. I'm
> still alone, still empty.

The next time the date of her death fell on Good Friday was in 2004, eleven years later. Moreover, 2004 was the year of the birth of my first and only child. Coincidence? Who knows if one life gone begets another just begun? The next Good Friday to fall on April 9 will be in the year 2066. I will be over one hundred years old if I am still around. In all honesty, it does not really matter. Each year on April 9, regardless of the day of the week, I remember her with a candle. Each year on Good Friday, regardless of the date on the calendar, I remember the crucifixion of my Savior and Luka's death. I take comfort in the fact that Sunday is coming and that the tomb is empty, for there is where my hope lives.

Other triggers in all shapes and sizes from out of nowhere will slam you with every feeling of loss and grief you thought you had overcome. Many occur at the seemingly worst possible times. They blindside you and will knock you down repeatedly, no matter how much time has passed! It takes strong people to face their own mortality and that of the ones they love, not shying away from the reality, for there are things we cannot change; they can only be carried with us.

I must admit, I do not understand it, nor do I wish to pretend to. I know very little, but I do know this; my nonsensical questions often have none, nor need answers. What I do know is that life is here and now and is only lived forward. It has taken me many years to come to that realization.

> And the past is the past and that is what
> time means and time itself is one more name for
> death. (C. S. Lewis, *A Grief Observed*)

After All These Years

It has been over twenty years say what, WTF? I thought to myself.

I held the white business-size envelope in my hands, staring at her full name in black letters and my current home address below it. My eyes glanced to the upper right corner of the envelope where I read the red text "AARP" and the business address below. My mind screamed in the silence of the kitchen. I tentatively tore open the envelope to reveal an invitation to become a member of the American Association of Retired Persons and a happy birthday wish.

"Happy birthday, really? She is dead! Oh my god!" I screamed into the silence of the room, thanking God that my wife and daughter were not at home.

I have moved eight times, changing addresses each time between three states, in the intervening years since her death. I changed jobs numerous times, remarried, and had a child. Oh, and by the way, she would not even be old enough to join the club.

Still with all the data that is collected by corporations and the government about our personal lives, they somehow miss this. Social media tracks our every keystroke. Then they sell our personal information to the highest bidders for profit. Google a word, just looking for information for your child's school project, and suddenly, ads for products show up on your timeline and in your email, unsolicited.

It makes no sense at all. They can track where we go, what we buy, and to whom we converse with. It is all public record, and I am living a very different life. Yet mail continues to arrive addressed to her at whatever is my current address at the time. Tell me if you can how any of this makes sense, and truthfully, should it matter at all? We schedule our days, and the world around us seems to revolve on a schedule. Life goes on, and life wrecks us right on schedule.

CHAPTER 13

We Choose the Scars We Will Carry

We are all broken but sometimes, oh yes sometimes,
the broken pieces of you and me
come together beautifully.
—Mark Wayne

Time is a curious thing. It does not care whether we care at all, whether we acknowledge it or not; it just is. The moments slip by; the seconds become minutes. The minutes become hours, and hours become weeks and days. On and on it goes. We cannot stop it, nor slow it down.

I drifted into and through my thirties and into my forties. I moved on, or so I showed the world, doing what I had to and wasting time as the sands in the hourglass that marked my time here on earth continued to fall. I was lost most of the time and oblivious to my being lost. I remarried in my early thirties, had a child at forty, and moved on with life, a life that was as far from the dreams of my heart as I could get, for truthfully, I was scared, scared of an unknown future and a past that haunted me. C. S. Lewis starts his book *A Grief*

Observed with the statement that the feeling of grief is very similar to the feeling of fear, and I have to say I completely agree. We carry that feeling of fear as we carry our grief, for it is not something you get over.

Broken Windows

The wind and rain outside fell lightly as Luka and I headed to bed. Just another typical thunder and rainstorm moving through the area. As the night wore on, the wind and rain picked up while we slept peacefully in the dark and the warm comfort of our bed.

The crash exploded in the darkness, a million shards of sound that penetrated the night. Luka screamed as we were jolted awake, our hearts racing. I was on her in a flash, covering her body with mine to protect her as I whispered "Shh, shh, it is okay" when in reality, I was just as startled as she was. My mind raced at the sound that had awoken us both. Our breathing was rapid, and all I could hear was the wind and rain pelting against the windows and the side of the house.

"What was that?" she whispered in a frightened voice.

"I am not sure, but it sounded like glass breaking."

Our thoughts went to an intruder inside the house; my senses alerted. With my arms still around Luka, I looked over her to see our dog, RC, who was sitting up on his bed looking around inquisitively.

"I think we are okay," I said. "RC seems fine, not worried. I am going to check."

"Are you sure?" Her voice carried an obvious note of fear.

"Yes, it will be okay. Pretty sure the sound came from just outside our window here."

"Please be careful."

"I will."

Our bedroom was on the back of the house with two windows, one facing the backyard, the other facing our driveway leading to the detached garage. I slowly and carefully climbed out of the bed. My bare feet felt the coldness of the wood floor as I made my way over to the window facing the driveway.

With my fingers, I slowly slid apart the window blinds, peeking through the plastic slats into the dark night. The outside light centered over the single garage door glowed in the darkness, and I could see the water droplets running down the window glass. As my eyes began to focus, our large tree in the yard across the driveway was dancing in the wind, its leaves and branches swaying back and forth as if to some song only it could hear. The shadows cast on the ground were images of writhing figures going back and forth dancing in the dark.

I peered through the glass, my eyes moving back and forth. A reflection caught my eye just below me. Looking down, I saw the twisted metal frame and shattered glass pieces all over the ground just below the window. The glass shards cast ethereal reflections of light in all directions dancing off the droplets of water from the falling rain.

"Looks like the storm window. The extra glass piece fell out and shattered on the driveway," I said.

"Oh my, are you sure?"

"Yes," I replied.

"Okay, come back to bed now. You can deal with it in the morning."

There is no way anyone could ever put that back together again like it was. It has been broken too badly, I thought to myself as I turned and walked back to the bed.

This seemingly inconsequential event in our lives foreshadowed my own shattering a few years later. When Luka died, my world was shattered, and nothing prepares you for that. There is nothing in the world that can prepare you for the empty box that a life leaves behind. In an instant, I suddenly became a widower, something I had never ever even considered.

I have carried my pain as a testament to her and our love, a beacon shining bright that I hid deep inside. For so many years, it was my only purpose, and yet I would not allow others to see this pain. I buried it deep, nurturing it and keeping it alive in the recesses of my heart, for selfishly it was mine. As dragons hoard gold in mountaintop caves, my greed burned bright for I needed this pain and grief to give my life significance, realizing I could continue to choose to be alone even in the midst of new relationships by closing myself off.

On the other hand, I could choose not to be alone. I could choose to reach out to serve others, to share my story, to shine a light into the darkness; that is my choice.

Death is scary; the end is something we rarely talk about except in polite hushed tones. Others do not want to hear about my experiences for that will only further serve to isolate me. However, death follows life as summer follows spring and winter follows autumn. It is the next dance of the party and a reality we all must face. It is something we do not have to and should not have to face alone.

I carry scars, some visible on my skin, others deep within my heart. The scars are real, and the reason for their existence is real. It all happened to me. I am the same person, and yet I am not. The moment of her death fundamentally changed me, and the story I chose to tell is my choice.

I believe we should try and consciously create a positive message from these experiences so as not to allow the suffering to overwhelm the possibilities. My journey has been unique to me. My entire adult life, I have struggled to place my own experiences in some kind of context. It colors what I show to the world (my heart I show to very few) and shadows my memories and the hope that still lives inside of me, for the invisible scars remain and...

> Sometimes the scars are angry
> Sometimes they scream
> Sometimes the scars bleed
> Sometimes they whisper
> And sometimes the scars...are just what we need
> Each jagged line
> Each memory it marks
> Each time we remember
> Our past is gone forever we are told
> We are left with tracks embedded deep within our souls
> Sometimes the scars are angry

Sometimes they scream
Sometimes the scars bleed
Sometimes they whisper
And sometimes the scars…are just what we need

What is the story you tell of the scars you carry, the pain you have endured? You can change the story you tell. It is your story, and you have the choice to tell the truth.

Starting Again

I am anxious about starting again, where and how to begin, wondering if it will at all resemble the image I hold in my mind, and yet there is always an excitement of starting something new. Is not every sunrise a chance to start again?

The beginning. We so often, I included, hesitate when starting something new. *The fear of failure, and even success, hinders our courage to reach out for something more.* I know staring at the vastness of a life before you can often be overwhelming.

The fear. It keeps us bound, the what ifs and buts that haunt our thoughts. Our own self-doubts assail our best intentions of doing something great. We stand at the door afraid to knock; we stand at the edge of the cliff ready to fly, wondering if we have wings.

The courage. Is inside of each of us via that still small voice. A small light will always illuminate our dark if we will let it shine. *If only we would take that first small step.* We begin, and failing, we remind ourselves, is not as bad as never trying at all.

Carpe diem. Begin right where you are right now. Follow your path, seek and live your life, slaying the dragons that will undoubtedly cross your path. *Allow yourself to fall, to fail, to wonder, to question, and to live without regret.* You never know; the journey may be even more beautiful and wonderful than you ever imagined.

I have wandered through many years of my life searching, and I often ask myself, "What are you searching for?" "I am not searching for anything really, I am running!" I reply. "Running from what?" I then ask.

I instantly rattle off the following, for there is so much in life from which it is often easier in the moment to run from.

- pain
- hardships
- loss
- success
- failure
- love,
- and even death

I have found myself running from all of the above and so much more, and for what? Only to arrive safely at heaven's door. Is that all there is? Shouldn't there be so much more?

We run from the life we could have, and we miss the adventure, the passion, the love in front of us.

As we seek, we must still ask the questions. The silence is so often the worst part. It is the ever-present, never-ending nothingness and stillness covering everything. The only sound is the clicking hands of the battery-operated clock hanging on the wall, each click marking time that means nothing because there is no answer to the questions that race through your mind. After a while, you know that there will be no answer, even before the question forms in your brain. Nevertheless, you ask it anyway, repeatedly, still hopeful that somewhere and sometime, there will be an answer.

Is not the definition of insanity doing the same thing over and over again and expecting different results? What is real? We ask while adrift in a sea of wandering and wondering. So many questions haunt my mind. Often it is the pain still carried which reminds me I am still alive, and it is not over yet.

The pain has a purpose, and grief is the happiness you experienced before. Wounds can heal, turning to scars that serve to remind you where you have been and how far you have come. For you, yes, even you, as we all are meant for so much more than just ordinary!

The way before us is yet unformed and filled with anticipation and expectation. Go forth and seize the day. Rise up like mighty warriors and face your fears. Slay the dragons and live the life that you imagined, chasing the dreams and desires that God has placed specifically inside of you. You matter—your life matters! You are a difference maker in the lives of others, and they need you. That is your destiny!

Promises

"I wanna know. Will you remember me when forever comes and goes?"

We have all made promises to do this or that, promises we swore we would keep forever. In the end, forever comes and goes. In the end, left alone, we hold onto the empty promises. Perhaps we broke our own promises with our own hands. Either way, I believe the question remains that haunt each of us. Will you remember me?

We must hold onto truth despite our feelings that would lead us to believe otherwise.

It is difficult when the things of this world so easily wear us down. Our hearts are broken and scarred from the constant barrage of evil that comes, and hope often seems so distant. Despite your circumstances and the things this world throws at you, will you continue to believe, to live with belief and a hope that better things may lie ahead and are sure to come?

> Has this world been so kind to you that you should leave it with regret? There are better things ahead than any we leave behind. *(C. S. Lewis, The Collected Letters of C. S. Lewis*, Volume 3)

If you could have seen the end from the beginning, would you have chosen a different path? For hope can still live as long as our hearts are still beating, and even after that, for death is not the end.

C. S. Lewis is right; death matters to all of us. Our own and others' physical death is inevitable, no matter how much we may choose to ignore it. I read that loving and grief are joined at the hip, and I agree. All the joy and sorrow that each brings, this is love.

Faith was all I had, and for so many years, it never seemed enough. Faith in a far better place—isn't that what Jesus promised? However…there are always the doubts of what I couldn't even put into words. She was simply gone. She was alive and breathing one minute, and then dead the next, her body becoming cold and stiff. She lay in that stark hospital room, upon those stark white sheets, the hue of her skin slowly fading to the same color as the sheets.

> Only those who will risk going too far can
> possibly find out how far one can go. (T. S. Eliot)

It is time to put every utterance of faith and belief to the test, to see if what I said I believed was what I really believed. There is this hole; it just got very real, and we choose the scars we will carry in this life and possibly into the next.

CHAPTER 14

As the World Moves On

I look up at the night sky. Is anything more cer-
tain that in all those vast times and spaces,
if I were allowed to search them, I should
nowhere find her face, her voice, her touch?
She died. She is dead. Is the word
so difficult to learn?
—C. S. Lewis, *A Grief Observed*

I came home so many nights to an empty house—I hated that. It was hard to be with people because I always had to come home. Nights were hard, but so were some mornings as I woke and would be blindsided by loneliness. I never saw it coming, or I just refused to look. The house was so empty, so stale, and so stagnant. I almost hated being here, but that was where the memories and her presence were the strongest. Even the air felt almost dead.

Nothing looked wrong, but the whole feel of everything was wrong. An undeniable feeling in the air covered everything. What could I do to fill up the empty spaces? I looked at the clothesline one night, and it looked so wrong. Then it hit me; only my clothes were hanging up, none of hers. Just my clothes, one set of dishes, one towel hanging in the bathroom—one can be the loneliest number.

I have touched on the fact that there are stories we tell others and ourselves about the wounds we carry, stories that linger long after the events have passed. The details of the stories morph and change over time, but the main themes and the feelings they evoke remain. My scars are invisible to most as they reside within my heart and mind. You cannot see them, and you would never guess the path I have walked when you first meet me. Maybe if you looked deeply into my eyes and truly heard my words, you might guess something was amiss. Suffering knows no bounds and is no respecter of persons, gender, or race. We all must endure pain in this life, some emotional and some physical, each injury unique in the pain it inflicts and how we, in our own ways, chose to deal with it.

As my mind wanders down the roads that have brought me here to this point in my life, I sometimes still wonder if it all is just a dream. I am content with my life now in the present, chasing new dreams and accomplishing things I never thought I would. I was there to the end when she took her last breath, watching helplessly as she died. I live with the hard truth that nothing I could have done would have saved her.

There are two stories I have told and continue to tell myself about her death and my pain, loss, and grief. Now after many years, both stories still carry elements of truth. The reality of trauma and grief of any kind fundamentally changes who we are and who we will become. How could it not? Traumatic events are the forks in the road of our lives that often lead us down paths we never intended to follow.

I have lived for many years with the belief that my loss and pain meant that I was different from others. I told myself it was useful in isolating and protecting myself. Yes, we are all different from one another, uniquely fashioned, a masterpiece in the Creator's hands. However, we all suffer, we all hurt, and we all face loss and devastation while searching for joy. Our stories and the circumstances of our trauma are different, no doubt, and yet the grief we all face and feel after the loss of someone we love is universal, a shared human experience.

I have often felt alone, wondering in the dark of a quiet bedroom late at night, silently asking questions that most have no answers, screaming inside that no one feels the way that I do or understands the depths of my pain or the love we had and that which was lost. To understand the shared human experience, there must be connection, sharing our different experiences in an effort to help others, for that is where relationships built on vulnerability and transparency thrives, for we are all broken, living in a broken world.

Good men have something to offer. I have nothing for I am broken and hurting, not famous. What good can I share with the world? Can our brokenness be a source of power to help not only ourselves to heal through offering of help and comfort to others? We look to those who have suffered and persevered in the face of trials and adversity. We admire their courage, and we love them for their resilience and find our own strength that we can also move forward.

It felt somehow disloyal to share my story, my love for her, and the pain I have endured since she died. I never wanted to be the tragic loner, the reluctant hero that others might pity and believe was weak if I shared my doubt and pain. However, if we are all broken in some way, might others find strength in my story of hope and perseverance in the face of loss and pain?

It's All Shit

I sit here on a quiet Sunday morning, only a week removed from a two-week adventure to Yellowstone National Park with my wife and daughter, and it all seems like shit! If I am being honest, that word fits—shit!

My blessings are many, I know that. I have a family that loves me, friends that care, and so much more. Opportunities have come, and I have worked my ass off at times, sacrificing to accomplish what I have. Looking in, one might say I am moderately successful, at least by the world's standards.

So why, as I sit here on the other side of my life's mountain with possibly less time before me than behind me, do I feel this way, and not just this day but on a lot of days? I am trying to embrace the present while still feeling:

Stuck! Marginalized! Lost! Uninspired! Disconnected! Lonely! Fatigued! Discontented! Overwhelmed! Anxious! Uncertain! Afraid!

I have dreams. We all do. Some taunt me and haunt me. And the question lingers: what good is a life that leaves nothing behind? I want to let go of the expectations of others, the responsibilities of the person who others think and want me to be.

It is all so exhausting. So many times, I feel I have lost myself. Oh, there are moments, real and true, that speak of a greater reality, and they are just far too few. I often wonder who am I meant to be. The past still haunts me now in the present, and there is a melody woven through my life that sings, if only I would stop and acknowledge that truth.

My dreams of passion and purpose dance at the edges of my days before quickly fading into the duty and obligations that chain me. I want to make a difference in the lives of others and shine a light into the darkness, the darkness of the human heart.

My self-imposed obligations and responsibilities weigh me down. So much drowns out that still small voice inside that would inspire and lead me higher as my courage fails me. I feel so grounded. What good is a bird with useless wings? My search, for what I often am not sure of, seems so fruitless and empty. I do not hear from God, a voice crying out in the wilderness. I only hear the silence of the endless heavens as I stare at the night sky.

I have spent time traveling and camping, visiting some of the most awe-inspiring natural wonders ever created, seeing wild animals in their natural habitat and yet…I wonder, is it the simple things, those random fleeting moments that comes unexpectedly in our days, moments that touch our hearts' desire and leave a lingering feeling after they are too quickly gone? Then we crash back to reality, wondering, hoping to recapture those moments of magic that do not, will not, and cannot last.

Is that where the bullshit often lies?

I stare into the darkness of my heart, knowing that I cannot change the world. Yet the world has changed me through my experiences. One cannot avoid the inevitable changes that will come after standing so close to death and walking through grief. I am not who or how I used to be.

I hear a still small voice whisper; maybe, just maybe I can help one person who can then help another. Ripples, you know? Is that what life is about, each person uniquely created to fill a certain destiny that only they can fill?

Why does it never seem to be enough? My doubts, fears, and insecurities well up, of letting others down and not being good enough, not being perfect enough. Perfect enough for what is the question.

Can good enough be good enough?

I realize there are more questions here than answers. I have spent a majority of my life asking these very questions, struggling to find answers as I attempt to live in the present.

Oh well…it is time to get my ass up, put on my jeans and dusty cowboy boots, carry a flame, and bang that drum for myself and others. One small, seemingly insignificant pebble can start a landslide, sending out ripples as it silently falls through the dark depths of anxiety.

God is not done with me, and I will trust in my time of uncertainty and silence.

It's Still All Shit (Part 2)— and the World Moves On

My thoughts turn as I watched the autumn weather change from the overcast of gray clouds to blowing winds and sideways rain, to the clouds suddenly breaking apart to reveal splotches of blue beyond the gray curtain. Then snow. *Really, it is snowing*, I think to myself as the snow quickly changes back to a drizzling rain.

Soon the sunshine slowly peaks out, playing hide and seek, then disappears, and the sky again begins dumping buckets of raindrops the size of marbles and then back again to clear skies of forever blue and bright sunshine. Over and over, it does repeat; round and round it goes as the world moves on, and is it still all shit?

We cannot be everything that everybody wants us to be!

Hell, sometimes we cannot even be what we want to be! These fears still haunt me into this present day. They invade my dreams while I sleep and taunt me from the moment I wake, never leaving me alone. These voices in my head that scream condemnation walk beside me each day.

There are doors swinging open and opportunities that beckon, and yet…I am often so confused. The ideas and possibilities swirl around me in a chaos of hurricane winds and in flashes of lightning that carve the midnight sky, leaving me tired. *Does anyone care?* I silently scream while I sit here quietly and watch the seconds tick slowly by, distracted by nothing and everything all at the same time.

My thoughts are a mess; my heart skips beats to a rhythm only it can hear as I wonder at the absurdity of it all. There is no choice but to embrace the only absurd choice that is available. She is gone, and here in front of me are choices and wonderful opportunities.

- Do I dare? Would you?
- Do I have the courage? Do you?

It takes tremendous courage to believe in hope when our faith is as small as a wisp of smoke, a single light far off in the dark, that is all. It can be a small thing that keeps us going before our hearts stop beating, while we keep hearing the banging sounds of drums repeating.

The world has gone mad, each person, each mother's son, everyone! There is hate and evil, remorse and regret, an eternal tag team we meet to do battle in the ring of our hearts. This ugliness and fear seek to devour our souls as cruelties unfold.

Mercy, grace, faith, hope, and *love* are all that can stand against!

Our lives are brief as memories linger, and the finality of death often overshadows the past. Nothing makes sense. Our memories of yesterday are quickly gone, replaced by the current tragedies seared into our brains through social media and the six o'clock news.

We need a lifeline, a belief in a hope that does not disappoint. With future memories of what could be, we see a light in the dark, a beacon of hope, and a reason to go on. The world will move on, and we will find ourselves repeating the refrain, *"It's all still shit!"* Once again, each day I find I am simply trying to regain my clarity and purpose, listening for that still small voice.

Luka and I are no longer journeying down this road of life together. We have not been for quite a few years. She, without meaning to or wanting to, turned off that road when she got the news of cancer in her body. It left me and others to march along our own roads as if we will be fine. Jenkinson, in his book *Die Wise*, talks about how we all must journey down these roads. From that moment, I began to sing my song of grief. You do not talk about it, but you began to learn about it. Grief is not my goal; it is a way of going on when it seems I am not able to.

Jenkinson goes on to say it is an uncommon understanding of love, this love that glimpses its inevitable end. "Until death do us part?" It is not approving of the end, for this is not necessary, but we love the world and life anyhow. This is how we unwillingly say a courageous faithful amen to the way it is, which is what acknowledging death asks of us.

To rebuild my life, I would have to let go of death, moreover, to carry the experience, all the devastation, hurt, loss, and anger right alongside the gratitude, the memories of joy, for the love and the pain, the joy and the sorrows forever occupy the same space in my heart, to discover where it is that I come from, knowing that death will always follow me.

Part 3

REDEEMING
THE FUTURE

CHAPTER 15

The Judgment of a Bad Man

*So speak and so act as those who are to be
judged by the law of liberty. For judgment
will be merciless to one who has shown no
mercy; mercy triumphs over judgment.*
—James 2:12–13 NASB

Days drifted into months as summer came into high gear. I would wake up alone again; my prayers for God to take me while I slept went unanswered. I hated the feeling that she was drifting further away.

"It seems you want the pain."

I stared, stunned by the words. I held my breath, my mind spinning with thoughts of do I lie or be honest. I took a breath and replied with anger.

"That's right, I want the pain! The pain is the only thing in my life that is real and honest. It hurts, but it is real. Don't you get that? Everything else in my life seems so unreal. Now that Luka is gone physically, the pain seems to be all I have to hang onto anymore!"

I still recall the days when the house was quiet, and I had the day off from work. You could already feel the heat rising, another hot summer day, and I would find myself making breakfast for myself, alone again.

The egg is slowly cooking in the skillet as the yellow yolk stares up brightly like the sun encircled by clouds before I stab the sphere, sending yellow streaks into the white surrounding it. The egg spatters as it cooks, and I deftly sweep the spatula under the egg and flip it over to cook on the other side. Egg sandwiches still remind me of you, but sometimes, it still seems that everything does.

There was always the void that swallowed everything, lurking in every corner of the house that haunted my steps. The quiet only made my mind spin faster. Early mornings seemed sometimes the worst because there were no distractions. I had all the time, and nothing to do with it.

I seem to remember that you told me I had a little boy inside of me. You always told me you loved me and not to be concerned with what other people thought. In the midst of your own battles fighting cancer, you were still concerned that I would be okay. We rarely if ever spoke of the possible inevitable ending, instead choosing to focus on hope we both clung to as our only lifeline. I remember sitting down at the table alone one summer morning. I turned to an open page in my journal and began to write.

> Dear Luka,
>
> I've been told that writing to you in this journal would make me feel better somehow. Well, I'm not so sure about that, but I'm willing to give it a try. It's called grief management techniques. In case you didn't notice, that's a department I could use a little help in.
>
> See, the thing is, I can't really believe that you're gone. I waste a hell of a lot of food 'cause I always forget that you're not here to eat some. I get in the car and wait for you to get in. I go to bed and wait for you to come. Sometimes I just sit, thinking if I wait long enough, you'll show up.

I am walking around, and people look at me like I'm a normal guy, but I'm not. Half of me is missing, and I don't know what I'm ever gonna do about it. I was never so mad at you while you were alive. But I am now 'cause you left me with this void. It's called my life.

Sometimes I think a baby of ours would help. I feel guilty and long for that sometimes. But even a baby would not make up for the fact that I'm, I'm so alone without you. To tell you the truth, Luka, all that strength you made me feel, well, it's gone.

Sometimes I do not think I am going to ever get it back. That is how I feel. I am angry, mad at you for leaving me alone. I remember once asking you if you were dying on me...

(I believe I wrote this based on something I had heard from somewhere, and I changed it to match my own situation, but I do not remember from where.)

I can tell that my writing in my journal ends here before continuing sometime later that same night. I know because there is a space between the entries, and I had used a different colored pen.

The song "Home Free" came on the radio, and I froze. I sat motionless, the pen still in my hand, listening, the lyrics penetrating my brain as I silently screamed.

If you are so good, why did you take her and leave me alone!

I prayed and prayed, and it did no good! She is gone!

Bull, every prayer does not get answered, no matter what they say!

I screamed and stomped around the kitchen, falling apart. It took several minutes, and I was able to compose myself, enough to sit back down at the kitchen table, putting pen to paper again.

Oh god, that was scary. That's the closest I've ever felt that I was actually losing it. I felt so out of control, so helpless, so scared. I thought my mind was going to explode.

I just sat and cried in the corner of the kitchen. Too much reality. I felt like I was going insane.

Calmer now, my heart is still going. Nobody, I mean nobody, knows what I am going through. God, I hate this. Am I going crazy? My head hurts, I just don't know what to do. No strength, and I'm no good to anyone, to finish what I started before.

You looked me straight in the eyes with your beautiful blue eyes and said, "No, I am not going to die."

Why did you lie? I'm mad you left me all alone with this void, this incredible emptiness that is now my life.

The journal entry haunts me and my accusing her of lying to me when in truth, I do not believe she intentionally lied. Looking back, I now question what she believed. Did she say no just to try to protect me? Did she truly think she was dying no matter what we did? I put her on the spot with my question, and I wonder why we do not speak truth about our fears and doubts to others, especially those who are dying. If we are the one dying, should we not also be completely honest about what is happening to us as we are dying?

I asked a question that haunted my heart and begged for an answer, or at least confirmation, of the answer I already held in my heart. A question that remains, is there any mercy for each sin committed that I have forgotten? Is there forgiveness for every temptation and every thought that rattled in my head over the years? Is there forgiveness for the acts done to try to fill the emptiness and to satisfy the lusts of the flesh seeking comfort, if only for a moment of respite? I still contemplate the desires that sometimes roared. I still consider these questions these many years later. Do the thoughts make the man good or evil?

What Good Is a Life?

It is a hot summer day; the campground is quiet. I sit in a lawn chair outside our camper, just praying, resting, and enjoying the silence and solitude before my wife and daughter will join me the next day. The sun is high above, a huge brilliant yellow against the solid blue, as I let my mind drift. A light breeze blows as my mind lifts upward, taking me out of this particular place and time into the heavens.

As I float ever upward, I look down to see the moment I have just left. I try to look forward to what may be, and I only see darkness for the future is yet untold. There is a story—my story, your story—that he will reveal to each one of us only in his good time.

To my astonishment as I turn to look back behind me, I see the world below me. Stretched out in the distance is the whole of my life retreating from this moment. Each event and dream, each success and failure is laid bare before me to see.

I look at the timeline of my life, trying to make sense of it all. These are not just random occurrences but interrelated events. They build on one another in a world that cries out that there is no purpose. I stare hard, my mind in a whirr when I see moments that seem to rise off the ground slowly above the rest at different points in my life.

I see some grand events of spectacular fashion with a significant impact. Other actions are only small gestures of a simple touch or a singular word, each instance either encircled by a radiating golden light or shrouded in a gray fog. The light and fog both mask the details hidden therein.

Justification by reason, the thought leaps into my mind. Each golden-lighted thing is an arrow shot straight into the enemy's heart. Each gray dart pierces not only my own but God's heart as well.

I tried so hard to do what I could—to help, to comfort, to support, to pray, to believe, to never give up hope. To each darkened thing, my eyes are drawn, those times I failed, stumbled, and fell. Of my own free will, I made decisions to forgo the basic human nature to help and be in the service of others.

My beating heart thumps loudly in my chest. I see the judgment that is to come, and I fear I failed each test. I think to myself, *What good is a life that leaves nothing behind.*

I am that man I dreaded I would be, a bad man who has hidden for years behind the mask, and his recompense are still to come. There are things I know, hidden deep inside, that would horrify others if they knew, my own dirty secrets and evil turnings inside that I carefully hide. I am a bad man, and bad men deserve to die.

Good men, heroes of the legendary stories, always save the day. They rescue the princess, slay the dragons, and they live happily ever after. Occasionally, they even sacrifice all by giving their own life, tragic heroes on a grand scale, and we love them even more.

I thought and believed I would give whatever was needed to save her life, whatever act or sacrifice was required. Yet this choice was never before me despite my ignorant pleadings.

To say you will do something takes on a vastly different meaning when faced with the reality of actually doing it. It is one thing to say you can face the hangman's noose or willingly walk the plank until you feel the coarse rope scape against the skin of your neck or your bare feet against the wet wood as the watery depths swirl below you.

I look back and pray I did everything I could to save my young wife's life from the cancer that ravaged her body, everything I could to heal her body, making the quality of her last days the best it could be. I stood by her side as we explored the many different treatments, conventional and alternative, each promising their own ray of hope.

Each moment, I stood next to her, giving her my strength while she endured the procedures. I prayed and sought guidance from both God and others.

I carried my load and tried to carry hers. So many seemingly menial things of caregiving that she looked to me, that I did—cleaning, cooking, and chauffeuring, all those things to keep the household running. Then there were all the things tied to her treatment and the physical limitations she endured—cleaning bandages and wounds, flushing catheters, helping her out of bed, into the shower, getting dressed, and even help going to the bathroom. All of this, and still I watched as she weakened in body, sometimes in mind and, eventually, to any future in this life. Her body tired and worn out, she died.

So the question that haunts me to this day is, was there something I missed?

A real hero would have found a way. Is not that what the world tells us? A real man always saves his princess. So logically, it follows the enemy continues to whisper relentlessly in my ears that I am not a hero or a real man, only a fake and a bad man. Bad men deserve punishment, so I, for many years, have punished myself in so many ways.

To pay this sentence, I have ordained myself as judge, jury, and executioner. I do not deserve the happiness, the contentment, the joy that I so desperately seek. I deserve damnation and hellfire because I failed her, because I tell myself I am the villain of this story I have been telling.

Renouncing the Dragon's Fire

Is the story I tell true? Is this only a manifestation of survivor's guilt? Is there truth in the minefields I tread? These questions I have grappled with endlessly, some days more than others, but I look behind me, and I see the footprints of guilt and doubt that follow me into my future.

I did so much for her, for us, when I know so many others may have run. I know this because I have had other men look me in the eye and say they do not believe they would be able to handle this and not run. Even a couple who did have a wife die told me they did not stay, and they have guilt about that. They pulled away emotionally, and some even physically, choosing to leave their princess alone to face the dragon with no one to fight for her. I did not leave physically; nor I believe emotionally, I stayed to the end of her last dying breath as the dragon's fire covered us both.

Still I hear a voice that says I failed her. I failed myself, unable to fulfill all the promises and vows I had made. I missed something, some small thing that could have saved her. The voice whispers I failed this test, and with that comes consequences. I have lived many days of my life with the veiled hope to see her again on the other side of the undiscovered, going through my days with my unspoken regrets.

I have reasoned each day that my moments of joy and happiness have to be justified with penance. There is no innocent fun given with grace, only the payment for crimes committed that weigh me down. It is only recently that I have renounced the vows and begun giving them back to God.

The Bible records that wherever Jesus went, people cried out to him, especially those shunned by society, the outcasts and the rejects, those who had lost all hope the things of this world, in others and in any ability to save them.

> As they were leaving Jericho, a large crowd followed Him. And two blind men sitting by the road, hearing that Jesus was passing by, cried out, "Lord, have mercy on us, Son of David!" *The crowd sternly told them to be quiet, but they cried out all the more*, "Lord, Son of David, have mercy on us!" And Jesus stopped and called them, and said, "What do you want Me to do for you?" They said to Him, "Lord, we want our eyes to be opened." *Moved with compassion, Jesus touched their eyes; and immediately they regained their sight and followed Him.* (Matthew 20:29–34 NASB)

Is this still true today even after 2000 years? When we are hurt, lost, and without hope, is it only then that we cry out to God? I wonder if in those moments, if those who profess no belief in God also find themselves calling out to God.

What is telling is the response of Jesus. He stopped, called to them, then simply and directly asked, "What do you want Me to do for you?"

The God of the universe did not indicate that He already knew what they wanted. He asked and waited for them to answer. In those moments as they stared into the eyes of Jesus, what thoughts were running through their minds as He simply waited for them to respond? When others had always dismissed their pleas and cries for help and mercy? Here now before them stood one who acknowledged their request and stood patiently waiting for them to answer.

Could it be true that Jesus, often in a still small voice, is asking this very same question even today, especially to you and to me?

"What do you want Me to do for you?"

My own fear has often kept me from asking, fearful of the response. The blind men knew exactly what they wanted Jesus to do for them, "Lord, we want our eyes to be opened." Clear and straight to the point was their answer.

It is easy to believe the lies of the enemy, the world, and our own minds. As our hearts spiral downward into the futile, a sweet poison is the penalty for sins repeated and each one we have forgotten. I believe that on the wings of love, we can rise from the ashes and the darkness deep, for there is forgiveness, even for those who find they are still believing the lies, regardless of the thoughts in my head that tell me I am a bad man, a complete screwup at times, or just a beautiful mess wrecked right on schedule, as he should be by what life has thrown at him.

Jesus tells us to forgive seventy times seven times, so logically, it makes sense that God would also forgive us at least that many times. I am thankful for this forgiveness as it allows me to continue to fight the whispered lies of the enemy.

CHAPTER 16

Holding Space to Dream Big

Dream as if you'll live forever.
Live as if you'll die today.
——James Dean

Watched from afar
by loving eyes of grace.
Angels stand silently
at attention holding space.
Ragged breaths float
into the fading twilight.
Limp soft hands
and open eyes without sight.
At God's command
quietly the angels step back.
Swords are dropped
onto heaven's floor——clack!
Cold and alone
shivering to barely stand.
The path before
leads into undiscovered lands.

Walking slowly away
into the solid darkness ahead.
Trusting paths unknown
through whispering shadows we tread.
An eternal light
will shine into our night's black.
If we choose to see
our future can be taken—back!
Answers lie unspoken
as new dreams emerge and begin.
Resting in stories
told of magic and truth without end.

On a recent camping trip while driving far into the mountains on a forest service road, my daughter found an unbroken clay pigeon. She was led to write a note to mark the spot and set up a marker, letting others that might pass that way know that we had been there. What really got me was that she added the words "Dream Big" at the end of the handwritten note. *Why?* I wondered. From the mind of a nine-and-one-half year-old the world is infinitely large, and everything is possible. For many years, she had been changing her mind almost daily about what she wants to be when she grows up, but her dreams have always remained big!

Her dreams have focused like a laser on horses, music, and writing as she has gotten older. Everything she wants now and in the future revolves around those three things. Although the details may change somewhat, her dreams remain big!

She has competed in equestrian performance events, worked hard on training her horse, taken trail rides, and dreams of maybe being a trainer one day. She takes lessons, plays the piano, acoustic and bass guitars, writes her own music, lyrics, and sings. She has written three novels in a historical fiction series that she intends to self-publish and writes poetry as well, hence the poem about grief at the beginning of this book. She sees the world as full of opportunity and promise. Oh, how I envy her at times.

The birth of my daughter has led me to realize that I walked away from many of my dreams. I do still dream, but they seem just that, only dreams which vanish upon waking, like fog with the rising of the sun. I have marked those milestones of failure and regret, much more so than my successes and joys. How different would the world be if we all pursued our dreams believing in ourselves? The outcome is not as important as the pursuit. I am into the second chapter of my life, with statistically less time left here on earth than I have been alive.

So now what, I ask myself. I am pursuing dreams, trying to send out ripples and shine a light into the darkness, both my own and others. If you also have walked away from your dreams of your youth or adulthood, it is time to rekindle those flames of desire. Your dreams of tomorrow and someday can ignite the fire that burns brightly your life of today. Let today be a milestone marker; celebrate it and dream big!

How often do we willingly seek the bright shiny objects that seem to lie so innocently in our path? Are these only random inconveniences of life or a devious plan to lead us astray? The things of this world so easily seduce us. I know as I have found myself on those paths littered with shiny objects that only serve to distract me from my true calling and purpose.

To quote or paraphrase C. S. Lewis, "the sweet poison of the false infinite" lures us temptingly toward always wanting more. I pray that each of us may hear that still small voice that whispers truth to us, and we are able to resist the poison that is so sweet, and yet promises nothing. For when we fall, forgiveness gives us wings to rise.

I still hold out hope, for myself and others, that forgiveness will come, that we can forgive others and ourselves for wrongs committed, that recovery becomes less about moving on or returning to some kind of normal life as defined by the world and more about living with and hearing the truth of the wounds we have suffered and what it may teach us.

There is wisdom in pain, if we seek it with patient honesty. It had been over a quarter of a century for me, a journey of epic patience as the grief weaves it way through me, making its own kind of beauty. I still pray that this life of justification by reason will become one of hope by grace.

Words and Questions

I became a bereaved widower at twenty-eight years of age, a strange word, just like grief, death, died, and dead. Just speaking those words aloud and sometimes even thinking them makes something happen. Something shifts in the trajectory of our lives. The dictionary defines the term *widowed* and *bereaved* as follows:

> *Widowed*—verb: *past participle: widowed*
> 1. become a widow or widower; lose one's spouse through death.

> Widow—*noun*: widow; plural noun: widows
> a woman who has lost her spouse by death and has not remarried.

> Widower—*noun*: widower; plural noun: widowers
> a man who has lost his spouse by death and has not remarried.

> *Bereaved*—verb: *past participle: bereaved*
> 1. be deprived of a loved one through a profound absence, especially due to the loved one's death.

We bandy these words about without really contemplating their meaning. Often, the tragic events that inspire them sometimes become the fodder for comedians. We laugh at the morbid jokes, knowing inside the seriousness of those simple words and thanking God it is about someone else and not us.

> She died. She is dead. Is the word so difficult to learn? (C. S. Lewis, *A Grief Observed*)

We use the terms *lost, deprived,* and *absence* when the truth is they died. Their physical mortal body ceased to work, and they died.

They are not lost; if so, can we find them again? As if we have mis-placed our car keys, wallet, or purse, maybe we just need to look harder.

"Oh yes, many years ago, I lost her."

No. No, I did not; I was there at the end, the moment she died. I knew exactly where she was. I did not lose her. I was lost in my own confusion and pain, but I never lost her.

The dictionary defines *widow* and *widower* as someone who has lost a spouse by death and not remarried, so if we remarry, are we now no longer widowed?

And do we allow those words to sum up an entire life? As our life rolls on, in every single moment, day, month, and year after los-ing a loved one, we are still bereaved. The words are just labels we use. No matter what changes you make, it does not change that fact that they died, and you suffered loss. The pain and the grief never goes away, even when you commit actions that take you in another direction, such as remarrying. Grief is not something you get over with; it is something you carry with you for the rest of your life.

"It irrevocably changes you. How could it not?"

If we are honest with ourselves, we may be seeking connection and companionship in our efforts at correcting what happened to us, for the things that happen to us cannot be fixed, nor changed, only acknowledged and carried. Loved ones die, and we have to love our-selves enough to love them despite knowing they are leaving. Loving others can be both a blessing and a curse.

Love and Truth

When Jesus was asked what is the greatest commandment, he replied, "'You shall love the Lord your God with all your heart, and with all your soul, and with all your mind.' This is the great and foremost commandment. The second is like it, *'You shall love your neighbor as yourself.'*" (Matthew 22:37–39 NASB). There it is; love your neighbor, or others, as yourself. We find this small scripture repeated many times throughout the Bible.

- Leviticus 19:18 (NASB), "You shall not take vengeance, nor bear any grudge against the sons of your people, but *you shall love your neighbor as yourself*, I am the LORD."
- Matthew 5:43 (NASB), "You have heard that it was said, '*You shall love your neighbor* and hate your enemy.'"
- Matthew 19:19 (NASB), "Honor your father and mother; and *you shall love your neighbor as yourself.*"
- Mark 12:31 (NASB), "The second is this, 'You shall *love your neighbor as yourself.*' There is no other commandment greater than these."
- Mark 12:33 (NASB), "And to love him with all the heart and with all the understanding and with all the strength, and to *love one's neighbor as himself*, is much more than all burnt offerings and sacrifices."
- Romans 13:9 (NASB), "For this, 'You shall not commit adultery, You shall not murder, You shall not steal, You shall not covet,' and if there is any other commandment, it is summed up in this saying, '*You shall love your neighbor as yourself.*'"
- Galatians 5:14 (NASB), "For the whole law is fulfilled in one word, in the statement, '*You shall love your neighbor as yourself.*'"
- James 2:8 (NASB), "If, however, you are fulfilling the royal law according to the Scripture, '*You shall love your neighbor as yourself*,' you are doing well."

"How do you love your neighbor as yourself when you cannot love yourself?" I often ask this question as I wrestle with my identity. We base truth on our feelings, our emotions, and our circumstances, the things we can see with our eyes hear with our ears, or smell with our nose, something we can hold or something we can own. On the other hand, is it something more this journey of truth and what is truth?

To paraphrase the Grinch, "Maybe it doesn't come from a store. Maybe...perhaps...it means a little bit more!"

I believe there is a reality beyond what we can always see. It lies at the intersection of the physical and spiritual worlds, and then sometimes, when the veil is thin, we catch a glimpse, a glimpse into truth that allows us to see, if only briefly, the reality in which we live. For now, we must rest in the assurance of myths that hold an element of the truth and the narrow path upon which it lies.

Whether we believe it or not, the truth is still the truth.

If we would listen to the voices of myth, those myths of a God whose great power is more than anything we currently know. Believe the legends of a God who became man and walked among us with only love. He weeps for the lost and the evil in the world, but the tales hold the truth in the words they speak. May we each be strong, help one another, and stay on the path to the truth, for he and a greater future awaits us, if we dare.

Seeking Compassion

I am now slowly rebuilding my life on a belief and hope that there is a reason to the seeming madness of this world. I have since married a wonderful woman who loves me in spite of my fears and sees more in me than I see in myself. I watched the birth of our daughter, and I am cherishing watching her grow into a precious and loving young woman.

Now in what I like to refer to as the second chapter of my life, I wish to share the joys, the sorrows, the hope and maybe even inspire someone on this crazy wonderful journey that we call life. I believe in the *ripple effect*, touch one life, and you may touch the world. The world craves compassion, and we should freely give it both to others and to ourselves.

We must have compassion for each other and for ourselves. It starts with us, each one of us. We can only do the best we can, and often, that is good enough. You are more than you know! My belief is that compassion transforms lives in the midst of the pain that is real. It does no good to deny the pain or medicate it away. It is there, and it is okay.

Men especially are indoctrinated by the world, friends, and family to bury our pain. So, guys and gals, consider this my challenge to you. It is not too late to join in. You do not have to spill your guts—promise—but if you engage in life, real life, somehow, let the world know that you are putting something out there, why it matters to you, and then you add weight and your own unique perspective to the world.

Spread the word. We cannot do it alone. It takes a village, right? We really are stronger together.

The world needs compassion, every one of us, on a daily basis, and it seems like we all have enough to share. And yet…it seems that my own compassion so often fails, miserably. My compassion for others and for me so often is complacent and appears nonexistent. People infringe, blatantly so without concern, on my life and my agenda. I am offended and hurt. *How dare they*, I silently scream inside. The world is full of unintentional slights.

- They do not hold the door for me when they clearly see me walking up. It doesn't matter that my arms are empty and work just fine.
- They cut me off in traffic without signaling a lane change, then speed off. It doesn't matter that they may have just got a call from the hospital and their first child is being born or dying.
- They drive the speed limit on a beautiful curvy country road where dappled sunlight filters through the leafless trees. It doesn't matter that I am in a hurry to get nowhere fast as I impatiently tailgate, gripping the steering wheel tightly.
- They talk loudly in the coffee shop about recent struggles with their marriage and child. It doesn't matter that I am frantically trying to type a blog post on my laptop that I know will change the world.

- They ignore the pain that I see daily in the mirror reflected back at me in my own eyes. It doesn't matter that I am oblivious and ambivalent to the silent pain I see in others.
- They stand staring blankly at me on the street corner, sign in hand. It doesn't matter I think; the light is going to change, and I don't have time as I sip my five dollar coffee drink.
- I call myself all sorts of vulgar and ugly names, berating myself for who I am and have become. It doesn't matter that if anyone did that to someone I love, nothing could stop me from exacting my own vengeance.

I am guilty of each of these things, repeatedly, and I criticize and belittle others for these exact things, even if it is only in my mind, for not showing kindness as if that justifies my anger and resentment. We see moments of compassion amid the violence and hate all over the news and social media.

Maybe it is in the little things, and maybe it starts with me, with you?

> Some believe it is only Great Power that can hold evil in check. But that is not what I have found. I have found that it is the small everyday deeds of ordinary folk that keep the darkness at bay. Small acts of kindness and love. (Gandalf, J. R. R. Tolkien)

CHAPTER 17

Physical Beauty and Emotional Scars

Sometimes the words fade…
—Mark Wayne

"It doesn't look that bad."

"Really?"

"Really, just a scar right here that no one but me will see, and I still love you."

The conversation was brief, the first time it was just the two of us at home after removing the bandages that wrapped around her chest, over one shoulder, and back under her other arm. Her simple hesitant reply of one word spoke volumes of her insecurity, and I owed her the truth. Although I only told her part of the truth, yes, I still loved her, and yet the physical reality was shocking.

At twenty-five years old, Luka endured a radical mastectomy that removed her entire breast, the lymph nodes under the arm, and the chest muscles under the skin, leaving her with only one breast. My understanding is for many years, this was standard surgery and procedure at that time in the early nineties. The medical practice that was supposed to save her life left her with a wide ugly red scar that started from her underarm and ran jagged across her chest to her breastbone.

When I first saw the still long red incision that ran across Luka's chest, still raw, the skin held together with dark stitches where her breast was supposed to be, I found myself unintentionally repulsed by the sight. I wanted to turn away, but my love, or more truthfully, my morbid curiosity at the mutilation did not allow me to turn away. My eyes stared until I forced myself them to look up into her soft blue eyes that pleaded for an answer to the question every girl asks, "Am I beautiful?"

The sight left me in shock. It left me confused and not at all sure what to think. I never knew what to expect going into this but never in my wildest dreams dreamed of this, to love, marry, and have physical beauty corrupted by something inside of her body that you could not see, nor touch. Only now, I could touch the physical ugliness that had resulted; this shit just got real.

I could not, not look but cannot look; I do not want to see, but I see. I wonder why God chose me, chose her, when the result is a falling short of the beauty that society claims is the ultimate. Did God want this life for me?

The guilt inside my mind over these unspoken feelings covers me, washing over my being like waves on the ocean, and because of my disgust, I turn my head and look away. She was a beautiful soul with a body that no longer met the perfection that society wanted and demanded. I kept wondering, if there is beauty found in pain, and we erase all pain, do we also eradicate all beauty?

Luka lived the last few years of her short life with an ugly physical scar across her chest. I loved this woman with all my heart. I loved her laugh, and I loved her smile. Our love ran so deep that we both gave freely to one another. Because of this love and physical attraction, there is the spiritual emotional union that results from a physical connection that is like none other on the earth. For those last years, I lived with this perplexing dichotomy of love and hate, desire and repulsion.

Sometimes All You Can Do Is Live with It

I loved Luka, this woman for who she was, and hating her for what the world did to her and who it had forced her to become. What the cancer did to her and what it took away leaves me to wonder, was my hate and repulsion misplaced? She was the manifestation of the disease, not the cause but collateral damage. It left me to witness it with no explanation. Doesn't a man of integrity travel the path despite what life throws at him?

A good man loves with a kind of supernatural and unconditional love, and so I often found myself pretending. I would go forward claiming my love, hiding a shame, hiding my feelings of guilt way deep down inside, guilt that I did not live up to the expectations I placed on myself. My thoughts fueled my anger and shame that I could not be better. I rarely allowed it to surface for my thoughts were my own. She had enough troubles, so I never voiced them, and it is a burden I still carry in this life.

This question rattles as I think about my identity and the masks I wear to this day. There is a good man and a real bad man inside. I am trying to make up for all my failings, both real and imagined. I carried a love and desire versus a hate and repulsion, sometimes both still buried deep inside, a love and hate, a desire and repulsion of this woman who I pledged to share life with until death do us part, which I did. I often do not understand either feeling that wells up inside and those same feelings I carry to this day. Again, there are things we must carry if we are to go forward for we do not easily get over it, and they change us.

Looking back, I still feel like I let Luka down, that feeling that I let everyone down, all those who loved her. It all happened right there on my watch, and there was nothing I could do. I had promised to love her in sickness and health and all that. I had one job, one task, nothing else; that was it. My selfishness during the ordeal and the hopelessness I felt was like a tidal wave, leaving me soaking and shivering alone on the shore. Here, to this day, I stand, still soaking wet from the guilt and shame I chose to carry.

Battling Together and Alone

My mind recalls her scars, the multitude she carried, both physical and emotional, physical scars inflicted on her as she fought her way through this life and the emotional scars the battle left behind also. I also call to mind my own scars, the scars her death left across my heart, not physical scars but the emotional scars that resulted. We walked different paths through the years, silently together, yet alone as we both battled our demons.

Ugly physical scars remained across her chest after the surgery. The long jagged scar was always a reminder, a reminder that the battle may wane for a while, but the war was far from over.

The reality of how the surgery messed with her body image as a female, I failed to consider at any depth. I was young, so was she. My mind did not consider the philosophical ramifications then. The hideousness of this medical procedure that was supposed to address the issue and hopefully save her life just made her feel less than. I recall conversations and her comments that she felt less than the ideal, less than perfect, less than beautiful, and less of a woman. I would shrug, tell her I still loved her, and it was okay, believing in my naivety that this banished all her demons.

We often made light of it. We joked about it. I think that was the only way we could both kind of put it into perspective or come to terms with it. Graveyard humor, you might say, because it was the reality we both were living. I also believe it was her graceful way of comforting and softening the blow of reality for me.

Luka found herself a young twenty-something woman with only one breast, me, a twenty-something young man who married a woman with two breasts who now only had one after only two and a half years of marriage. Neither of us expected this when we signed on as young lovers who married in our early twenties, but who does?

Now I wonder was she, even while battling her own pain, trying to protect me? I know it was extremely difficult for her. I can only imagine the pain, the emotional pain that she felt that lingered long after and beyond the physical pain inflicted by the surgery. We trudged forward while she dealt with her pain, and I dealt with my own emotions.

If this saga had played out with a reversal of roles, she would have handled it so much better than I did. But it didn't, and I tried to be a good man, but I so often felt cheated and sucker punched by the hand I was dealt. A wife with only one breast—but isn't a marriage and relationship so much more than just the physical? I would try to convince myself while languishing in my own self-pity. While she silently pined away, I often left her there in her loneliness and pain.

My own struggles blinded me often to her needs. I struggled with my own emotional pain of loving her and desiring her physically. The physical desire of wanting to be with her sexually and to comfort her remained because I loved this woman. Then out of nowhere, the moments of hate and repulsion would erupt when I would see the physical scar, catching me off guard again. I had forgotten in the midst of daily living, but once more there's the reality.

As she turned or undressed, the reality would raise its ugly head again, and I would scream inside to God, *Why me!?* and *I don't know what should I be doing!* We can love despite a disfigured human body, for love transcends every physical sense. Then there was the pity that I felt for myself, without thinking of her. You know, the "why me" moments of selfish desires that foist upon me the shame of my failure.

She was young, and now she was so different from what the world tells you physically she should be as a female. Yeah, societal acceptance of a feminine form and the feminine beauty and all that it is not is tied up in that. It was just so very, very hard to view a beautiful creature that you had fallen in love with now changed; it was the reality.

Then there was the logistical issues of, you know, the bra with pouch sewn in, a pocket where the gel prosthetic would go in. After the physical recovery from the surgery, we visited a specialist to help with the visual aspect of seeming perfectly normal. They did measurements for the right size, the right-size bra with the right-size cup to match her one remaining breast. The prosthetic was made of gel, inserted into the bra pocket to make her appear "normal" when covered by clothing. Two breasts, isn't that what God intended when he created Eve from Adam in the beginning?

Every night, we placed the prosthetic gelatin insert in a box for storage and handwashed the specialty bras. It was all always a pain to deal with, to think about, and a daily reminder of the seriousness, but she was alive, and we learned to live with it.

As time wore on, we more or less accepted our fate, or so I thought. The graveyard humor surfaced time and time again. We even invented a game that we would joke about, attaching a strip of Velcro on her chest and Velcro on the back of the prosthetic. I, as the contestant, would toss the gelatin blob at her chest. She would stand still as I tried to get it to stick in the right place. We never actually did this, but we laughed about it as we acted it out, and it eased the tension a bit. It was all just a joke to try to make things a little lighter when faced with the reality of the situation. She laughed and I laughed, but it was not a laughing matter, and I know now, sometimes moments of levity occur during the worst of times. I wonder now if she was just playing along, again trying to protect me.

Then there was the aspect of hiding this from others, especially in social situations and when she did not know the other person. She had one side of her chest with a normal breast. The other side of her chest was completely flat, and her clothes just hung over the spot of the missing breast if she was not wearing the prosthetic. It was definitely never more so than when she was in a swimming suit.

The last few months of her life, we spent hours in the hot tub in the backyard as it eased her pain to be weightless in the water. When Luka was in her one-piece swimming suit in the hot tub, the cloth of the swimsuit material just hung there. You could tell something was just not right, that something was missing, another reminder that I could not change or fix. It was just wrong and so off center in so many ways.

I tried and so often felt like I was failing to love her the same way as before, and I did not know what to make of that. She was different now, both physically and emotionally, and she did not know what to make of it. This was just the result of the cancer that apparently had always been inside her body. God, if it really were that simple, but our minds tend to complicate matters.

The surgery left a physical manifestation of the damage—the scars, both physical and emotional, and the everlasting scars that life left her with and she took to her grave when she died. The emotional scars, I can only imagine, must have seared her heart and mind, just completely made her ask her own questions of God.

Created in God's image, created in the image of God, male and female, and then you end up looking like this. God does not have a body he is spirit, so we are made in his image in spirit, yet we live our lives in a physical world. This had to be harder on her than I will ever know and messed with her head and something that I have no idea how she dealt with to this day.

Now I am married to a woman with two breasts and have a daughter. Both of them may face the same fate someday that befell Luka, a disease that affects many women as the search for a "cure" goes on. I wonder at this as they say those who learn nothing from history are doomed to repeat it. Not that I have anything to say, whether such a fate will befall either one of them, but the question remains if it does, did I learn anything and how will I deal with it?

The best is perhaps what is understood
least. (C. S. Lewis, *A Grief Observed*)

CHAPTER 18

Death Feeds Life, Children

Today was a good day Daddy, I didn't get hurt.
—Muppin, age 6

"You know you will be a great mother someday."

The words had tumbled out of my mouth before I knew what I was saying, and I instantly regretted them. The day was warm and sunny. We talked idly as we waited, and I realized in that moment this young lady standing next to me, with the bright sun reflecting off her dark-brown hair that hung down past her shoulders against deeply tanned skin was who I wanted to spend the rest of my life with.

"Thanks," she said, and I could instantly tell she was uncomfortable. It was still early in our relationship, and we had never talked about either of us wanting or having children before, although I knew that she loved them. Children, they were Luka's joy and her sorrow. Luka had been working off and on at a local day care and had shared with me how much she loved it. She loved the children, and they loved her. She was a mother and a friend to so many little ones. She showed them love, grace and taught them right from wrong on so many occasions.

"Really, I mean it. You are so good with kids, and the kids at the day care love you," I said, trying to regain some semblance of order and settle the uneasiness that hung between us.

"I know," she said as she shuffled her feet on the pavement. I detected the hint of sadness in her voice.

"What's wrong?" I asked.

She hesitated, turning and looking off into the blue sky, so I waited as cars drove by on the street, oblivious to two young lovers in the midst of a conversation that could change the entire trajectory of their relationship. I waited, my stomach full of fluttering butterflies, and after several seconds, she turned back to me.

"You remember I told you about my Hodgkin's disease I had when I was younger?"

"Yes," I replied, holding my breath.

Taking a deep breath, she continued, "Well, the treatments I had, radiation and stuff. The doctors said that it would most likely cause me to be sterile. I won't ever be able to get pregnant. I probably can't have kids."

Finishing, she looked away from me. I stared at her, contemplating what she had told me. This moment that occurred over thirty years ago is frozen in my memory. The words she spoke then did not, I recall, faze me at all. *So what?* I thought. I was young; she was young. We had our whole lives ahead of us. I wanted her, the moment, the now, not the offspring that she was now telling me she could never have and I would never have with her. It was prophetic, and I dismissed it. Again, I wanted her. I was not concerned with the what ifs, the maybes, or even the nevers.

"So what? No big deal. I love you." I smiled as she gazed off into the distance, confused as to what she was thinking. Luka continued to look away, and I stammered, "Really, I mean it."

Turning back, she looked at me and smiled, a hint of resignation in her eyes as she took my hand in hers. That conversation was a turning point in our young relationship and propelled us forward. We had come to a kind of mutual acceptance and understanding. I knew there was no one else I wanted. In that moment, my mind followed my heart, and my decision was made. I wanted her to be my wife someday, knowing that children for us would probably never come, and the grass was never to be green in that area of our lives. Little did I know how the weeds would grow so quickly to overtake that patch of ground on which I had staked my future.

We only briefly entertained the thought of adoption some years later after we were married. Yet, every time, it seemed there were medical or financial issues we're facing, and the time was never right.

Vivid memories of that conversation came back late in the night just before she died. I sat on the edge of her hospital bed. I felt the torment haunting me that she was fading, and soon there would be nothing left of her to hold. I would never see her smile reflected back at me in a smile from a child. Far too soon, she was gone; I was alone, my arms empty with nothing to hold. Yet that memory and her words would ring in my mind repeatedly as time marched on.

"Momma, don't be mad at him..."

The words rang in my head like a banging cymbal. Thoughts of anger, sadness, and complete confusion swirled in my mind. After what my daughter had experienced, how could she say something like that? My wife silently stood, watching and waiting as I struggled with my thoughts.

Well, I thought to myself, *My little girl is better than I am. That is for sure.* She has more compassion in her little finger than I have in my whole body. We talked more about the situation, ultimately deciding to wait a few more days before making a final decision. After all, she was only in kindergarten and seemed okay, this despite the repeated occurrence of the little boy putting his hands on her neck and squeezing until in her words, "she thought her eyes might pop out of her head."

This young girl was our miracle baby. With Luka's words ringing in my head that she might never be able to have children, my wife and I had been trying to conceive for over five years.

She was small and petite, one of the smallest in her class and an easy target for the bigger boys of the same age. Taken out of school was not what she wanted as she had many friends and enjoyed her teachers. We had spoken to both her teachers and the principal so they were aware of the incidents that had occurred. They assured us they would keep a close eye on the little boy to make sure these types of things did not happen again. It was only two months before the summer break, and if we could get her through, it would be okay. However, a few weeks later, our little girl relayed another story that happened in gym class with the same boy.

"He came up behind me and picked me up and dropped me on my head," she calmly stated to her mother while holding her head at an angle because of the pain in her neck. "Momma, don't be mad at him. He doesn't know any better." Her little blue eyes were sparkling like crystal as she gingerly moved her head, her blond hair swaying around her neck.

Numerous trips to the chiropractor, and the pain in her neck lessened. It appeared there was no long-term damage. However, the headaches continued, and no amount of chiropractic adjustments helped because the stress remained. She was worried, as we were, that this little boy would came after her again. My anger flared. I was ready to confront the parents of this little boy, and only calmer heads prevailed.

We continued to struggle with the decision to pull her out of school or not with only a couple of weeks to go before summer. My wife was exploring homeschooling and seemed determined to convince me that next year, this was the best option for our little girl. I remained unconvinced. Although I would do anything to protect my little girl, I also wondered if this was something she needed to learn to deal with and not let the bullies win. I did not want my only daughter to believe that she was a victim and live her life not standing up for herself.

I picked her up from school one Friday afternoon. We buckled ourselves in, and I started the car, turning to look before backing out of the parking spot. Glancing in the rearview mirror at my beautiful blonde little girl, I asked, "So how was your day today, honey?"

She smiled and looked back at me. My heart fluttered seeing her face in the mirror. She stated with a touch of joy in her voice, "Today was a good day, Daddy. I didn't get hurt."

Before the words had died in the air, my heart broke, and I did not know how to respond. I felt the immensity of the moment and the familiar helpless feeling that I could do nothing. I swallowed hard and mustered a reply. "That's good, sweetie."

There was nothing about school, her friends, or the fun that she had; no, the best part of my six-year-old's day was that she did not get hurt. *Are you f—— kidding me!* I screamed in my mind.

Fighting back the tears, I began slowly backing up the car and silently drove home. That night, my wife and I decided to get her through the last few weeks of this school year. We would explore homeschooling for the next year when she entered first grade. After much research and many conversations with our little girl over the summer as this would affect her also, we made the decision to home-school our daughter, and we have never looked back.

Luka could not have children, and I accepted that and married her anyway. We lived and loved until the day she died and left this earth. Years later, after falling in love again, my wife and I never really wanted children. I was dealing with the conflicting emotions still, with loss and being true to Luka. I was okay with us not having children, or so I thought, and I thought so did she. We spoke the words that we did not want children. As the years went, by our words began to lose their power. Thinking we might be running out of time as neither of us was getting any younger, we began trying to get pregnant. *Why not,* we both wondered, and still I harbored some fear and anxiety over the possibility of being a father. I mean my thoughts went to, was I being unfaithful to Luka since she could never have children?

After five years of marriage, then five years of trying to get pregnant and numerous false alarms, including fertility drugs and intra-uterine insemination (IUI) techniques that did not work, we gave up, figuring we were not to be blessed with children. I figured that was just the path in this life I had to follow. Then it happened. God had other plans, and my wife got pregnant. At the age of forty, I became a father to a beautiful little girl we affectionately refer to as our miracle child because she is. She grew, and the circle keeps coming full circle and maybe, just maybe, God has an impeccable sense of comedic timing.

How Do I Make Sense of This?

Every once in a while, here in the present where we live, something occurs that drags the past blasting into the moment. It shatters the moment and sets the stage for what the future could be, those rare moments that cross over, splitting through the veil between the spiritual world and the physical world.

My young daughter was ten years old at the time when she drew a portrait of Luka who died in 1993, long before she was ever born. After I returned home from work one evening, my daughter quietly slipped into our bedroom and left a piece of paper on the bed for me to find. In a shaky ten-year-old hand, my daughter had drawn a figure, a likeness that comes pretty close to capturing the physical look and, even more so, the soul of Luka, and my daughter never had met her, nor seen a picture of her.

In the preceding weeks, by overhearing comments between her mother and me, she had deduced on her own that her daddy might have been married once before. When she came out and innocently asked the question, we did not want to lie to her, so we told her the truth, minus many details that a ten-year-old does not need to know. We (I) had always planned on telling her someday; just figured it would be on my timetable, not hers. It is not within our powers to keep certain secrets, and so it seems God will reveal then in his own time.

It rocked my heart. This little girl has continued to exhibit more compassion in her young years already than I will ever hope to have. My daughter cares deeply and has told her mother she does not want to make me sad, but she also wants to know all about this woman who was part of her daddy's life before she was ever born. I have puzzled over this turn of events, more nonsensical questions I suppose. I keep coming back to this picture drawn by a ten-year-old girl of a woman she never met who was a huge part of my life when I experienced tremendous joy and, ultimately, some of my darkest hours of pain in life so far.

The phrase "How do I make sense of this?" kept going through my mind. Well, God moves in mysterious ways, and it occurred to me that maybe, just maybe, this is a way he is bringing deeper healing to places in my heart that I still refuse to go, a reminder that there is death, and whatever it is matters. Moreover, whatever happens has consequences, and it and they are irrevocable and irreversible as C. S. Lewis says.

I love my girl and her momma with all my heart. God has blessed me beyond measure, and my gratitude often goes silent and unspoken. I pray I learn to love deeply and honestly, like my little girl and her mother, who choose to love despite the cost it can bring. She and her mother are my muse and inspiration. May we all choose to believe that grace wins and hope lives, and yet things will still happen that will shatter the foundations of our lives. I puzzled over the seemingly random event that occurred, all the while believing that it was anything but random and wrote the following poem.

> *How do I make sense of this?*
> *It leaves me breathless.*
> *As I stare into the dark abyss.*
> *I am unsure how I should feel.*
> *A life now transcended.*
> *Could this be another path to heal?*

CHAPTER 19

Wrecked on Schedule

There is death. And whatever is matters. And
whatever happens has consequences, and it
and they are irrevocable and irreversible. You
might as well say birth does not matter.
—C. S. Lewis, *A Grief Observed*

Death matters, and you never ever get over it. The passage above from the C. S. Lewis's book *A Grief Observed* is haunting and so true, at least in my case. I have read his small book *A Grief Observed* many times, losing count since reading it for the first time in the summer of 1993, shortly after Luka's death. As I read, my mind wanders down the roads that I have travelled, eventually bringing me here to this point in my life. I sometimes wonder if it all is just a dream. There is death, it matters, and it wrecks everyone on schedule.

Every April is another anniversary of her death at the age of twenty-six from metastatic breast cancer. The early spring weather is often unpredictable and always a stark reminder of the grief I carry and the ultimate fragility of life. After Luka's death, I was a young man left alone, carrying a suitcase full of dreams and questions that clamored in my mind for answers. It is often the absolute cold silence in response to the questions that haunt my mind, even more so, like shadows that can never be grasped. There are often no answers this side of the undiscovered.

I felt left with only two options following the diagnosis of cancer and, eventually, after her death. The first and easier path was to hide and shrink from connection with her then and with others and the world now. I have chosen this option many times, and still do even now these many years later.

How often do we hide, camouflaged if you will, from others and even ourselves? The false image we present to the world will eventually become our reality and then color everything we know and are. This is not truth but a lie and although seemingly the easier way, I for one do not want to live this way.

Openness to the inevitable pain of life is difficult. Transparency is rife with trapdoors, and there is fear in being vulnerable, not to mention the ridicule that can often come from others. Our hearts need protecting, yes, but also our true freedom may only be found in healing the broken places we all carry deep inside.

The questions continue to beg for answers, questions that keep us awake at night when the distractions are few. How do you see yourself? How do you believe others see you? What is your truth? Will you drop the camouflage and emerge into the open, or will you continue to hide?

On the other hand, the second path is to dream, create, and pursue new visions yet unformed. The future, my future, was suddenly a blank slate filled with opportunities and choices, most I had never asked for, nor wanted, which only served to overwhelm me.

I lost my purpose and vision in my late twenties when Luka died. *What was left?* I often thought to myself. What was I now to do? Where was I to go? My life, the life I had envisioned, and the purpose we had been pursuing together now seemed wholly inadequate and inconsequential. It was the two of us, not just me, so those dreams we dreamed together of the future were now just like a book that was read long ago and placed on a shelf where it sat unnoticed, collecting dust, forgotten.

That book of us with stories of our life together and so many still empty pages was now a relic of the past, my past. It just did not make any sense to return to that story, for the ending had come. There would be an epilogue, if you will, that would now be a prologue to a new story. I needed to forge my own story, keeping my relationship with Luka, for death does not end it, but it certainly changes it.

Rituals and Traditions

The details of different cultures regarding death can be fascinating and unsettling at the same time. An interesting article titled "Death Is Not the End: Fascinating Funeral Traditions from Around the Globe" by Kate Torgovnick May explores a few different funeral traditions that might strike someone outside a culture as odd. A Ted Talk by anthropologist Kelly Swazey titled "Life That Doesn't End with Death" explores Indonesian beliefs where big, raucous funerals are at the center of social life. Swazey talks of this culture in which the bodies of dead relatives are cared for years after they have passed away—because relationships with our loved ones don't simply end when breathing does.

All these different rituals and customs from different cultures are fascinating in and of themselves, for dying, must be an action, not a passive response to the inevitable. Dying is what we all must do, not allowing it to be merely what happens to us. We often refuse to talk about it in any particular terms, unless in specific focus or support groups where the lifting of the taboo of death occurs in small settings, if only for an hour at a time.

So this might be the most supreme, most sublime tragedy in the litany of miseries that so often is dying in urban dominant-culture North America: We stop trying to control our dying finally at the point when we have little or no stamina energy, give-a-shit, and time to give to the honorable and immensely necessary

project of dying well, dying lucidly and deliber-
ately, dying purposefully and surely and wisely.
(Stephen Jenkinson, *Die Wise, A Manifesto of
Serenity and Soul*)

The views of the majority of American society and the rituals
toward death are unique. American culture seems to me to be more
of one that often says, *the best thing you can do with death is to ride off
from it.* (P.S. I paraphrased and borrowed that line from the book and
movie *Lonesome Dove* by Larry McMurtry.)

Is this an American societal acceptance that you (I am speaking primarily about men here) never let others know the impact of
death? We attend a funeral dressed in black, speak reverently of the
dead, while perusing the food table, and then we quickly go back to
our normal lives, or so it seems.

There are no formal rituals in America that lasts from days to
months, even to the year anniversary that I am aware of, allowing
those grieving to celebrate the life of the deceased and come to terms
with the death of a loved one. We put on a solemn appearance for a
couple of hours one afternoon to attend a funeral and/or memorial
service, and that seems to be it. We applaud and congratulate those
who go back to work the next day and appear to get on with their
lives immediately after the loss. We say they have an inner strength
and are impressed with how well they are dealing with the dying part
of life. Speaking from experience, it is not that easy. We go on, but it
never leaves you. It's not something you just get over, and you carry
it with you every day for the rest of your life.

There are rituals brought to America from people of other eth-
nicities. In those small communities, the rituals live on, sometimes
swallowed up by the American individualistic ethic of the strong. We
should not wallow or stay in our grief, but the fact that many often
simply choose to ignore what has happened seems absurd. To grieve
or celebrate the life and death of a loved one, unless done in private
or as part of a larger scheduled and manipulated public event, seems
the only acceptable display? Are we not to share the individual grieving especially by men? Is that because we are uncomfortable with

others' grief and pain? Or are we uncomfortable with our own? Or both?

"All men die, and most men miserably" (C. S. Lewis, *Why I Am Not a Pacifist—the Weight of Glory*). If we substitute the word grieve for die in the C. S. Lewis quote, is not the meaning the same? We fail, we fail to die, and we fail to grieve when the time comes. Stephen Jenkinson, in his book *Die Wise*, states that it is hard as hell, it is counterintuitive, and it is mandatory that when the time of dying is upon us, we have to find a way to stop trying not to die. I would add also, it's the same when dying is upon those we love who are leaving. This statement is true of grief as well; it is hard as hell at times. To be good at it, to be good at hurting or suffering, what would that look like?

Angels, Demons, Ghosts, and Spirits

In the many years since Luka's death, I have never had an encounter where I could say without a doubt that a spirit, ghost, apparition, angel, or demon visited me. No supernatural visitation of my dead wife has occurred, although I believe in the spirit realm. The Bible records visitations of angels on humanity that were always met with fear and trembling. Therefore, to reason something more like doubt, anxiety, disorder, panic or chaos may be more of what a visiting angel might bring.

Demons on the other hand, the Bible says, can masquerade as angels of light and righteousness. The so-called happy visitations of deceased loved ones from beyond the grave assuring those left behind seem to me as suspect. Again, maybe I am jaded, since this has not happened to me, but my faith tells me that my grief is blessed, and all will be right one day.

I have had a few dreams, some recounted in other parts of this book, and I have prayed hard for some small assurance that Luka is okay. There was nothing, just silence from God and the simple phrase "trust me." I struggle, and yet my faith encourages me that hope still lives and to just believe. In those moments where I stand at the abyss of what is and what was, what could be or have been, it seems easy to make a choice to throw it all away and to search for her in all the "vast times and spaces" of the nighttime sky, if only to selfishly comfort myself in this physical world.

However, as C. S. Lewis states in *A Grief Observed*, "I should nowhere find her face, her voice, her touch. She died. She is dead." Not passed away or sleeping but dead. See, the words are not that hard to say. How can you prove love? We know it when we experience it, but…? Yet my faith carries me, so I live with my desires, both for this world and for the next.

> If I find in myself a desire which no experience in this world can satisfy, the most probable explanation is that I was made for another world.
> (C. S. Lewis, *Mere Christianity*)

Maybe we cannot find the dead, nor can they find us? We remain separated by the unknown, a vast undiscovered. We drift here in the physical realm easily disconnected from the spiritual realm. Maybe when we die physically and enter into the undiscovered, that is when the beloved dead who preceded us will then find us? Until then, we can dream and live the life before us.

I am content with my life now, chasing new dreams and accomplishing things I never thought I would. Still sometimes late at night in the dark or on a sunny day, a memory shakes loose from the attic of my mind. Grief rises up again, and I cannot help but wonder, is my life better than it could have been? A nonsense question maybe, I do not know, but I do know that my questions are not a sin.

I was there to the end when she took her last breath, watching helplessly as she died. I live with the hard truth that nothing I could have done would have saved her. My life now is so very different from what I imagined so many years ago and so amazingly good most days. I am happy and realize, despite some lingering survivor's guilt, that life, this life, my life, does go on if I have the courage to make that choice.

My memories are secure, albeit I am the first to admit maybe not entirely accurate or true as time has a way of reshaping our history and the recollections of days gone by. Most memories are beautiful and serene with the remembrance of a life and the love it brought into this world. I hold the memories close, resting in the simple consolation that nothing can take them away.

C. S. Lewis is right; death matters, to all of us. Our own and the death of others is inevitable, no matter how much we may choose to ignore it.

- If we choose life, we also choose death.
- If we choose love, we also choose loss.
- If we choose joy, we also choose sorrow.

It is not an option to have one without the other. We ignore death and its consequences, choosing to remain in our ignorance. Many appear to remain unaffected or touched by it until one day, it comes up and smacks us painfully in the ass and our hearts!

Death, a simple word really, only one syllable but containing worlds filled with promises, rewards, fear, mystery, beginnings, and endings. It is a reality and one that we all must face. Yet there are moments that occur which the memories of will linger and echo long down the corridors of our minds far after death wrecks us on schedule.

> The real man smiles in trouble, gathers strength from distress, and grows brave by reflection. (Thomas Paine)

CHAPTER 20

Trust and Granting Permission

The struggle is real. We reckon with who we are,
who we wish to be and who we were created to be.
—Mark Wayne

On one particular Good Friday not so long ago, the sun's early spring rays shone down as afternoon slowly began its fade to evening. A hot breeze blew off the water as we stepped outside on the sidewalk, leaving behind the coolness of the air-conditioned store. It was unusually warm for this early in the year. The bright sunlight and heat were startling after the cool darkness of the little shop. Beige-colored cones filled with hard ice cream were tightly clenched in each of our hands, the old-fashioned way. No frozen yogurt for us, no sir!

The sweetness of the cold chocolate slid down my throat as I licked the delicious frozen treat. The street was quiet, and you could hear the crashing of the waves on the distant shore, along with the occasional squawk of a seagull. All life's troubles and cares seemed to fade away with each lick of cool chocolaty goodness. I stood simply enjoying the moment, a seeming perfect end to a great day.

I brought the cone to my mouth for another sumptuous taste of the quickly melting ice cream. A small drop splashed on my thumb, and I jerked a little as it splattered. Turning my hand to lick it off, the softening mound of velvety chocolate slowly tilted from its perch atop the hard cone. The misshapen glob of ice cream slowly slid, falling off the cone and splashing onto my wrist before rolling down the inside of my forearm, leaving behind a stream of light brown as it stopped momentarily at the crook of my elbow.

I watched in horror as the misshapen mass of now soft ice cream tittered on the edge. I froze, everything happening before me in super slow motion as it hung there for a second as if suspended by an invisible string before gravity took hold. Still in slow motion, I watched as it fell through the air, until it collided with the unforgiving concrete of the sidewalk, chocolate splattering in all directions.

Standing silently still, I watched as the ice cream continued slowly melting into an ever-widening pool of liquid chocolate on the concrete. I could neither shout nor cry as I was lost in this moment when all that was important in my young life had seemingly and so easily slipped away from me.

The mocking laughing cries of the gulls at my misfortune broke through my reverie. I raised my head, tears forming in the corners of my eyes as I took a step to walk away. I was trusted with my own ice cream cone, and I failed as it lay melting in the sun. The music coming from inside the ice cream shop stopped me in midstride. I listened to the lyrics being sung over the sound of the gulls, "Oh yea, they say life goes on / Long after the thrill of living is gone." As I walked away, I thought to myself, *I just don't get it.*

Life moves on…we move on. We carry it with us. We do not leave it behind and still, to this day, I do not get it. Every single moment of tenderness and love and each moment of joy and sorrow stays with us; it is who we were, are, and have become. I am still seeking permission after all these years, to give myself the permission to live fully, to be happy and fully love again without limits, permission to enjoy, delighting and cherishing the moments, to feel everything and accept its inevitable ending will come. Knowing that the human heart was built to break, and when it does, as it will, the feeling is a way of remembering the deep things of life that need remembering.

Do we believe that he comes that we might have life and have it abundantly?

To Live Is Christ, to Die Is Gain

What? How is that? It has often seemed to me, at least in my own experience, that death often takes me further away from God, not closer. Death throws a silence over my faith, and so many things seem contradictory and so unreal.

God is good? Let's explore that a little. Can you truly say that when you have faced death, tragedy, and the destruction of your world? Can you say that and believe it when you have never faced the end?

- Watched helplessly as the final breath fades away?
- The death of someone you love?
- Your own mortality?

When there is no one and nothing to blame, is evil or random purposeless consequences the easy answer, or is it the only answer for the cause of so much pain in the world? The violence, the hate, the addictions, the lust, and the greed continue unabated, and good people get hurt because of it. Are we just collateral damage? Or are we all just innocent victims living a pointless existence with random occurrences? We spin the wheel of life, and sometimes the pointer lands on someone we love and, eventually, on us.

How do we respond to illness, a sickness and death with no concrete cause? We can point to so-called triggers and probable causes of cancer, and yet we still question why. Others in high-risk categories live long and seemingly healthy lives.

Was there a cause, an action that brought about the effect and the consequence? What is the grand design and meaning in that if there are no coincidences?

Do I blame God? Am I angry with God? Her death irrevocably altered my life. I say I still believe and I go through the motions on the outside, showing an image to the world, but inside…do I believe?

The face I show the world, is that the truth of me? Do I truly believe what I say I believe? When I am alone in the dark, what am I left with? Total, utter silence from God, or am I just not listening? There were no words from beyond the veil, except for a faint whisper of *"Trust me,"* but faith is the evidence of things unseen, right?

Why is my overriding question that remains unanswered. This question that still haunts my waking and sleeping, but no answer ever seems forthcoming. *"Trust me."*

- What is my faith in the finality of that? *"Trust me."*
- What is next for me? *"Trust me."*
- What about for those I now love? *"Trust me."*
- Is there something beyond this life? *"Trust me."*
- Is it there a heaven and a hell? *"Trust me."*
- Did she simply fade to black? *"Trust me."*
- Will I simply fade to black? *"Trust me."*

We must give ourselves permission to feel the fear, accept that loss and devastation that may come again. *"Trust me."* It all makes me tired, so very tired. Life should not and is not meant to be lived waiting for the hammer to fall. The days and the years go by, and the hole remains. You laugh and love again. The moments of joy you so desperately longed for returns but often failing to be fully present and to live in that moment because of the fear. We juxtapose the past, present, and the future. *"Trust me"* whispers through my mind while I feel a

- fear of God
- fear of loss
- fear of happiness
- fear of succeeding
- fear of failing
- fear of guilt
- fear of forgetting
- fear of hurting
- fear of love

"Trust me." Each day is another chance to give myself permission to live fully. *"Trust me."* There will come a time when despite all that happened, it is okay to be happy and fully love again. *"Trust me."* We wait for the permission to enjoy, to feel delight, to cherish, to feel everything, and accept the reality whether we like it or not, and it must be given. *"Trust me."* You are permitted to love God, to accept your destiny, your life, your fate. *"For Jesus said, 'The thief comes only to steal and kill and destroy; I came that they may have life, and have it abundantly'"* (John 10:10 NASB).

Living with the Silence

It is in the mountains that I find solace and distance both from the past and my present. I have been running, or pedaling in my case, riding my bike from my past and often from my present, unwilling to be transparent and vulnerable with those I love and care for. I am learning that running, or riding off from it, does not always solve the issue.

There is a silence around me as I ride. I can block out the world, especially as my tires roll over the gravel and the dirt down the trails through the trees, crashing through streams as my legs are pounding, my muscles burning. I push up a hill, crest the top, and gravity takes hold in the acceleration of flying back down, keeping your hands off the brakes and letting the tires run, trusting them to find their own way.

Bike riding in my life has been a constant forever, and I have never questioned that. I ride because I want to. It is my escape into silence from the obligations, expectations, and the other million responsibilities.

When I was commuting by bike to work during Luka's sickness, I arrived early one morning while it was still dark outside, probably six or six-thirty in the morning. It was a cold winter day, and another employee arriving asked me how I could ride my bike in this kind of weather and in the dark so early in the morning in January.

I remember looking at them and responding simply that there were so many things out of control in my life right now, but this is one thing that made me feel a little bit in control. This fellow employee was unaware of Luka's cancer, and I did not share any details. I was taking back a little bit of my power and control where I could get it.

As I ride, always pushing myself, I have this nagging feeling of something chasing me, although around me is silence. The thought of being prey ricochets through my brain, and I pedal faster, my stomach fluttering as my breath catches in my throat. *Oh my,* I think to myself as my legs continue to piston up and down. The ground rapidly passes by under the rubber of my tires as I speed down the trail, my hands gripping the handlebars.

I realize my pedaling is a form of running away, and I think that for all these years, the bike has become my vehicle of escape. It has become my mode of trying to run from everything. I find myself often still running, feeling chased by everything that happened to me: the loss, the pain, the helplessness, and the grief, no the matter how far or how often I carry the pain with me on every single ride. The grief is a silent unwanted passenger on every single trip and always with me when I return to where I started.

I live each day in the fear of losing those I love. It often terrifies me because I know it is inevitable. It will happen; I just do not know when. It is the possible reality because in one life, I lived that very reality, wondering why someone so young and alive could get sick and die. I have asked many questions of God over the years and been met many times by only silence. There are moments I try hard to remember and moments that I will never forget.

When we experience "silence" from God, we may doubt our faith and even the existence of God, told the lie that silence signifies a negative experience. We pray, we listen, and hear nothing but silence in response to our cries. We yearn for an audible voice to break the silence, to calm our growing fears and doubts.

Could God actually speak loudest in his silence? God does speak of his everlasting love, faithfulness, power, gentleness, compassion, sacrifice, righteousness, and grace. To hear that still small voice, we must quiet ourselves, remaining and listening with more than just our ears and believing that God's unending grace will be unveiled.

I believe we find God's voice in so many things—the silent rising and setting sun, a snow-capped mountain range, clouds floating across the sky, a bird soaring high overhead, a rainbow after the rain, the body of Jesus hanging lifeless on the cross, and the silent echoes of an empty tomb.

We tell ourselves God is silent, but often, he is not. We equate this perceived silence as his disappointment in our lives, and nothing could be further from the truth as he daily shares his wondrous creation and love with us. When God seems silent and distant, we should desire to remain there, captured by him.

As I grow restless in the silence, thoughts arise that I must seek the answers elsewhere. I remember Peter's response to Jesus when asked in the sixth chapter of John if he wanted to go away also. Peter replied, "Lord, to whom shall we go? You have the words of eternal life."

The answers I seek are nowhere else, so I will rest, captured, knowing that God's silence means this is not over yet.

Holding Nothing or Holding Everything

There is will power, and there is way power. There is holding hope and space for ourselves and for others. When we find ourselves wholly lost in the dark wood, and we stumble across a tin box sticking up out of the ground, of course, with an excitement, we would dig it up, brush off the layers of dirt and dust, only to find…"Nothing! Really? Nothing…?"

Our mind screams as our spirits fall at the emptiness of another failed attempt, standing here holding an old empty tin box, rusted and dirty, with no identifiable or distinguishing marks. Story of our lives, we tell ourselves. It seems at times we are always left holding something that is actually nothing. It can seem it never changes!

Time to move on, we tell ourselves. Stop wallowing in self-pity and regret. So why do I just stand here holding this empty tin box? The sun is beating down on my head, birds are singing in the surrounding woods, clouds float lazily across the sky, and the trees sway gently in the early morning breeze. The wild does not care if you cry;

it will take your pain and anguish, the screams of torment, and safely carry them for you if only for a while.

There is lots of simple beauty to be grateful for that surrounds me, and here I continue to stand holding an empty tin box containing nothing.

I don't get it. Toss it aside. Move on! Let it go. It is nothing and contains nothing! My mind continues to scream. I wonder, so…why am I holding onto it, afraid to let it go? *Just drop it*, I say to myself, but I cannot.

The emptiness of the box holds nothing and speaks of rooms that yearn for filling. To fill a space through a second chance we never wanted is our obligation. We must fill the gap that we hold in our hands as it sits there in front of us just waiting, wishing, and longing for us to move, filled with anything that we can dream of. The possibilities are endless—joy, love, laughter, adventure, hope…whatever we choose. I have a choice. You have a choice. And I realize then in that moment as I hope you will too. It may seem we have nothing when in fact, we have the whole world.

CHAPTER 21

You Never Told Me about This

My soul, wait in silence for God
only, for my hope is from Him.
—Psalm 62:5 NASB

The quiet all around was loud inside my head. I felt a sense of expectancy
in the air.

The breeze off the lake contained a slight chill. This was a welcomed
respite after the heat of the day. The small waves pushed by the breeze
lapped against the gravel-laden shoreline. The boardwalk was empty this
early evening. The wooden boards running vertically beneath our feet
showed the signs of the many footsteps of those who had walked along this
path and were well worn.

The diffused evening light cast a golden glow, settling over the land-
scape as the sun touched the horizon. The ground to both sides of the
wooden boardwalk was a stark bleached white from the powerful desert
sun. The winds that blew had stripped the earth bare, leaving it barren
and void of life, except for a few sparse trees that struggled for survival
anchored deep in the dry parched dirt.

We walked silently, me with my hands pushed deep into my pockets,
and her pushing her little bike forward, hands firmly on the grips, wear-

ing a mask devoid of emotion on her face. The sleeves of my white shirt were rolled up to my elbows, and I could feel the flapping of the shirttails in the wind as we walked. Her white summer dress hung loosely on her young body, a stark contrast to her brown, olive skin. The lack of color in our clothes matched the landscape as if we were a part of it.

Looking inland away from the lake, I could see the empty parking lot far in the distance. Ours was the last vehicle there; others were gone now, headed where, I had no idea. I only knew that they had somewhere to go. The loneliness settled over me like a shroud as my steps faltered, and the sun sank its lower half now hidden below the horizon.

Catching my stumble out of the corner of her eye, she knew better than to ask how I was. Instead, she simply stated, "I am tired."

"I know, sweetie." I replied as I quickly regained my balance and told myself she had not seen my misstep, nor knew the reason why. However, deep down, I knew that she knew. She always seemed to know. Her understanding empathy, the ability that came so naturally to her and guided her actions was far beyond her young years.

As we continued to walk, she said. "I just want to sleep, all the time."

"It's okay. I get it. If that's what you need, then that's okay."

The silence then settled around us again as we moved forward. We strode onward as if drawn by some invisible force that neither of us could deny. I knew she was tired and worn out, even without her earlier comment still echoing in my head. My heart ached, knowing I was powerless to stop the pain. I still found it hard to admit, even to myself, the conclusion I knew was inevitable and unavoidable.

Life is hard, and for her to learn this at such a young age seemed so unfair. My anger over the injustice burned; however, the sadness and longing overshadowed it like the darkness. I looked across the lake at the exact moment the last of the sun sank beyond the horizon into the undiscovered. Melodies of grace erupted in my head in songs of redemption and a belief in a light that will one day overcome all darkness. As quickly as the feelings rose, they disappeared as the despair again wrapped its arms around me, choking off my breath.

I felt so helpless and alone, my life and hers slipping from my grasp and everything I held dear. We continued to walk in silence, comfortable together in our solitude. Over the past few days, I had watched as she grew weaker, and I hated the fact that my little girl's strength was quickly fading, and I knew the end was near for us both.

The words came, from where I do not know, and spilled out of my mouth in a cry of anguish.

"I miss her. God, I miss your momma."

"I do too, Daddy," she said with a stark honesty that cut to my heart as tears began to form in the corners of her eyes.

We stopped walking. The bike lay on its side where she had let if fall. Picking her up, I held her close, feeling her wet check against mine. Our tears mingled together as they ran down our faces. Her arms tightly squeezed my neck in defiance of tomorrow and yesterday, for this moment was all we had.

The preceding story is not true. It is from a dream I had and has led me to the following thoughts which I will try to put into words that make sense. I believe we have all felt the arcing of life, the ticking away of the seconds, hours, and days that we will never get back, and the inevitable conclusion we all are marching toward, our death and the death of those we love.

Moments are all we truly have. There are no promises for tomorrow, next week, or next year. Time is finite; eternity is not, and our days here on planet earth are numbered. From the momentous—the births, deaths, beginnings, and endings—there are things we all must experience.

Over time, our memories can morph and fade until the reality barely matches our recollections. I know in my own experience, Luka was in her midtwenties last time I saw her. When she died, her body had only just begun to show signs of the effects from the unavoidable decay that comes with aging. I find myself here now a much older and different man than the one who at twenty-eight stood by her hospital bedside, holding her hand as she died.

I live an entirely different life, and many years have gone by. The few pictures I have are of a young woman, and those are the images in my mind. I know she would look very different today if she had stayed. I am glad the images and the memories remain. However, therein lays the fallacy of our memories. They morph and change until the memory we hold in our minds may no longer match the reality.

I have no photograph of her that's any good. I cannot even see her face distinctly in my imagination. Yet the odd face of some stranger seen in a crowd this morning may come before me in vivid perfection the moment I close my eyes tonight. No doubt, the explanation is simple enough. We have seen the faces of those we know best so variously, from so many angles, in so many lights, with so many expressions—waking, sleeping, crying, eating, talking, thinking— that all the impressions crowd into our memory together and cancel out into a mere blur. But her voice is still vivid. The remembered voice—that can turn me at any moment to a whimpering child. (C. S. Lewis, *A Grief Observed*)

Words Said and Unsaid

"Her biggest concern was that you'd be okay."
"Really?"
"Yes, that is what she confided in me. She didn't know how to help you, and she was always worried about you. She just never knew how to tell you because she saw how much you hurt."
A friend of Luka's during a conversation relayed those words to me sometime after her death. I remember listening to the words intently, for I knew Luka always cared, not because of anything I did for her but just because she loved me unconditionally. I knew that then without a doubt and have never questioned my belief that she did love me. Yet I wondered then, and still do to this day, were there other things she never said or told me?

Under a starlit sky, land of a forgotten day now lays
Full moon illumination, shows a rocky path ahead

*Down the ravines, past towering sentinels of
evergreen
Ancient mythical words, creation screams with
wonder
Whispers on the wind, words I cannot comprehend
Trying to speak, my tongue dances behind my lips
A vision of you, rises before in silent beauty
My heart thunder drums, the love I feel escapes in
waves
Lost inside my mind, you turn and quietly walk
away
To hear you speak, the truth when we believe the lies
No regrets, O'me, O'life…
There are words we both wanted to say*

I know I live with so many words left on my tongue that I will never be able to say to her, words of love, support, and encouragement, words of my truth and words that often fell silent because of my own fears, conceit, and self-importance.

Can we ever truly say enough? Words have power, yes, power to console, to uplift and to tear down and demean. Can words heal a disease that ravages a young and seemingly healthy body? Do our prayers matter only if they are spoken aloud and do not remain in our head? Are our prayers only wishes in disguise?

Is sitting in silence sometimes enough? Just to hold a hand in the midst of pain and suffering is no easy feat. No mere words can end that misery, only those spoken in true belief, and only God can then perform the miracle. A touch of a hand and a soft smile can be of immeasurable comfort. The union of two souls in the silence of the physical can breach the borders and walls of the spiritual. There is no satisfying explanation, only our experience of when and whom we are in the moment. Then you will most certainly know.

The world and its material trappings, obligations, and demands fade away, until two hearts beat as one in perfect synchronicity that for a moment all is as it should be, a connection that is so real and stronger than any three-strand cord.

Words—as children we are told to use them wisely for once spoken, they can never be taken back, encouraged and instructed to be careful, to be compassionate. As we grow, we see the power of words, the power to hurt others before they hurt us, a heady feeling of strength that is so true, only momentary in its effect for us, but the words spoken sometimes echo forever in the mind of those toward whom we hurled our attacking insults.

Words—well-intended but meaningless in their impact on the listener. There are words spoken only to placate the speaker for they have done their good deed for the day. The words, like smoke from a candle wisp into the sky, quickly disappear, words that can forever ring in the eternity of the mind, that offer no solace for often there is none in that moment.

"You'll be okay."

"It was just her time to go."

"You are strong."

"She is better off now."

"She is no longer in any pain."

"You are young. You'll find someone else."

"Just let me know if you need anything."

The worst is asking a person who is grieved if they need anything. Really, you have to ask. I had no idea what I needed, only that I would scream the words in my mind, "I want her back! Can you make that happen?"

Even in the depths of my pain and sorrow, I knew the truth that nothing this side of heaven could bring her back. The words spoken in well-intentioned moments of sympathy so easily float from the lips of those who want to help. Then after speaking them so quickly, drift away, finding their schedules unexpectedly full. "I am sorry. We can't. We have other plans already. Maybe next time."

Why would anyone be willing to sit while we thrash, scream, and cry over a life lost and dreams lying shattered? Over the pain and anguish that drums on endlessly? I often saw the discomfort in their eyes when I was having a good day. They wonder what is going on with me, a constant reminder that life is cruel sometimes and will deal its blow before the end, either the death of someone we love or our own.

What Dying and Grief Ask of Us

For us to grieve well is tremendously hard, for those that die that we love, both while they are leaving and after they have left. It requires strength, a physical strength, yes, but more so an emotional strength to acknowledge what is happening. It asks us to not push away our feelings of regret and shame but to live with gratitude for that which happens that in the moment does not seem to benefit us. We learn what to do with grief when it comes to us so we can proceed in life knowing that certain things are true.

I have struggled to learn this skill, often pushing away my grief and the accompanying feelings of sorrow, depression, and loss. Do whatever it takes to resolve our grief and get to the other side of it, we are taught. This often means ignoring and pushing aside our feelings rather than experiencing our sadness, a trustworthy achievement.

We should learn some of these things, whether we enjoy them or not, in order to do them well. Not so; we do not have to do them, or so we are able to quit doing them. Our sense of grace about dying, whether in youth or old age, and the accompanying grief can be a guidepost and belief that life is going on as it must. This is far beyond mere acceptance of some mundane fact of our existence, such as a change in the weather that dampens our spirits. This is love and loving life despite the troubles of our existence and proceeding forward with heart and hope.

We love despite our lack of understanding or lack of answers, and we shout praises and thanksgiving for the breath still in our lungs. We should not accept death for what it is or be fine in spite of it all. It means to be broken just as it is destined, to allow ourselves to feel both the joy and the sorrow for what we have now, for what we are losing, and what we have lost. We grieve while those close to us are dying, all the while not wanting them to die and telling them so. It means speaking the words while you still have the opportunity and wanting more than anything for them to not be dying. It means missing them long before they die and telling them so. It means sitting in silence and being unhappy with them about what life has thrown at you both, instead of only being sad about them after they are gone.

I did the best I could at that time in my life, and there was so much I did not know, the skills we all desperately need to help others who are leaving and grieving. However, I do believe she breathed a little easier as I held her hand until her last breath. I was innocent when death and grief came knocking. There is so much to learn, and no one had ever told me about this.

CHAPTER 22

Cowboys Aren't Supposed to Cry

Beware the warrior poet...
—John Lovell, Owner and Founder
of the Warrior Poet Society

I had lived through four months and a day since Luka died when I came to my first birthday without her. Another first in a year of firsts that is what a death brings. Every event and every anniversary since was another reminder that she was gone and not coming back. Each birthday marks us turning another year older, although it did not take a birthday to make me feel older; the day she died I felt as if I had aged ten years.

The summer had been long, dry, and hot days, and many long lonely nights. I found myself after four months, feeling that I should have figured it all out by now because that is what a self-sufficient competent man would do.

I needed something for me, something that I enjoyed. My life seemed to revolve around my conforming and confirming to others that I was okay. I had shut down emotionally, just going through the days in a state of numbness. Part of me felt guilty, but the larger part of me needed this. There is something about seeing life from the back of a horse. It can change your perspective.

Years earlier, my father had sold his horse, Blaze, to some friends who lived in Garden Valley, Idaho, a little over an hour outside of Boise. I arranged to go up the morning of my birthday and ride. Even the phone call took me out of my comfort zone to ask for something from someone else. It would be the first time I had been on a horse in at least six or seven years.

It was a typical warm early August morning, clear blue skies and a big bright-yellow sun overhead as I drove up into the mountains. I spotted him in the pasture as I drove up, and my heart leapt. Blaze seemed to recognize me as I approached the pasture, and he trotted easily over to the fence.

I scratched his forehead under his forelock. I immediately fell into an easy rhythm of the mountains, enjoying the silence around me. The anxiety in my stomach settled as I breathed deep the mountain air. I was alone in a place I never expected to be, a widower at twenty-eight years old, today turning twenty-nine.

Being alone here in the mountains with a horse was exactly where I wanted to be at that moment. Since I could not have her, here seemed the next best thing. Everything in my life had changed, and yet there was so much that was still the same. Blaze nuzzled me, pushing his head against my chest. Sometimes you just know when a moment or decision is right, and when those times happen, even in the midst of your world around you being dark, you rest in that assurance.

I felt the heat from the sun on my back and knew it was going to be a hot day, although it was only midmorning. I set to retrieving the blanket and saddle from the shed where they had told me it was. I begin to tack up Blaze. I relished the smell of the worn leather and even the horse as they took me to another forgotten place and time.

I was stepping out of my reality of the day job, bills, obligations, and loss into a space where none of that mattered for now. Blaze had always fought having a bit in his mouth for many years, but today, he took the bit easily without fighting it. I took this as another confirmation that this is where I should be.

187

I led him around the pasture at a slow walk, letting the saddle settle before retightening the cinch. Opening the gate, I led Blaze onto the dirt road that led up into the mountains. They had told me he had not been ridden in a while, so I wasn't sure what to expect. He was well cared for, no doubt, but a horse can get out of practice and be unpredictable if not worked regularly. They are a powerful animal, and a lot of respect can keep you out of harm's way. Taking a breath, I stuck my booted foot in the stirrup, grabbed the horn, and hoisted myself into the saddle.

I heard the creak of the leather beneath me as I settled down into the saddle, and I slid my other foot into the stirrup. Blaze stood calmly like it was just yesterday that we had been together. I sensed he knew me, and he knew I needed something only he could give. I sat quietly atop a horse I had known so well long ago in another time and place. Sitting quietly, an occasional buzz of an insect was all I heard. As the sun beat down, I let my thoughts and my spirit settle into the moment.

Blaze sidestepped as the flies buzzed around his eyes, and he stamped down, turning the dry earth into little clouds of dust under his hooves. The smell of the hot dry dust floated upward through the air. I could tell he was anxious to get going, but I held him still, and we lingered in the silence all around. For the first time in months, I felt a peace wash over my soul, and I prayed a little prayer of gratitude.

After a few minutes, I clucked softly, and Blaze easily started forward at a slow walk. I immediately fell into rhythm with his easy gait. The pace was hypnotic and soothing to my soul as the reality of the life I had been living slowly melted away.

I had always considered myself a cowboy even during those many years when I did not wear boots, nor was around horses. My heart burned for the open spaces, solitude, and the companionship of this magnificent animal. As Blaze walked slowly, I reveled in the silence and in the moment as my thoughts began to wander with more clarity than I had found recently. I wondered that the absurdity of life and how death is as much a part of it everything else. In addition, sometimes we must embrace the absurdities that come before us. Why are we so surprised by what life throws at us, whether we call it fate or an accident?

My Destiny

Being a cowboy, even if was only in my heart, is my story. In fact, the narrative goes that late in my mom's pregnancy, my parents traveled from the small coastal town of Florence, Oregon, where I was soon to be born to attend a rodeo in the town of Eugene, Oregon. As they sat watching the rodeo, they perused the day sheet of the upcoming events and the names of the contestants. As they looked it over reviewing the names printed in black ink on the paper, they came across one of the bucking bronco events. They saw a cowboy listed with the name of Mark Wayne. My parents looked at each other smiling and immediately knew that my name was to be Mark Wayne.

I was destined to be a cowboy before I was born. As I rode Blaze higher into the mountains, I relaxed to his easy gait and the slow rocking motion beneath me. The beauty of the forested high desert landscape overcame me. I was a cowboy riding a horse through wide-open country; no fences to impede our path.

The memory of my last ride on Blaze is still strong all these years later. As I recall the memory, my thoughts drift to the present and the future, turning to the cowboy movies I have always loved. Movie scenes, images, and dialogue float through my mind and have become a way of living my life. This story I have created for myself and have lived for so many years now.

In a scene in the movie *Lonesome Dove*, an accident takes the life of a young cowhand at the beginning of the cattle drive. The others cowboys bury him, and Robert Duvall's character, Augustus "Gus" McCrae, agrees to says a few words about how short life is, and it can happen to any of us at any time. Gus then says, "Boys, let's go on to Montana." The character of Woodrow Call played by Tommy Lee Jones then makes the comment that Gus is right, and the best thing you can do with death is to ride off from it as he turns away and mounts his horse. The camera pans back as each cowboy turns from the grave's dirt mound covered in rocks and, without a word, mount their horses and restart the herd of cattle pointed north toward Montana. This is what we often do with tragedy and pain, especially men; we ride off from it.

Another favorite movie of mine is *Open Range*, starring Kevin Costner and again Robert Duvall. The scene shows the two men lying on their bedrolls, staring up at the stars, a small fire between them to ward off the cold of the night. Costner's character speaks of things he has done in life and ends with this, "Every once in a while I almost get through a day without thinking about who I am and what I'd done." It's a typical trait that we push aside our feelings and get on with the job at hand, yet so many of the things done and undone haunt our steps in life.

In the John Wayne movie *Big Jake*, during the big climatic fight scene at the end, Wayne's character, Jake, is rescuing his kidnapped grandson. During the ensuing gun battle, as the two of them hide behind a pile of straw, thunder booms across the night sky, and the boy jumps into Jake's arms. He asks his grandson "You scared?" and the young boy simply answers "yeah." Wayne's character then says to his grandson "So am I, but do not let them know it" as he turns back to the ongoing fight. This is sometimes necessary in the midst of the fight, and yet we will push down those feelings of fear so deep as to never admit this to anyone.

The movie *Quigley Down Under* with Tom Selleck has a moving scene that shows a cowboy's true heart. Earlier in the movie, Crazy Cora's character, played by Laura San Giacomo, tells the story to Matthew Quigley, Selleck's character, how her husband rode away from her and did not look back following the death of their son. In the sequence, Quigley is tacking up his horse to head off in the early morning to finish the fight when Cora steps out of the house. Quigley, leading his horse, walks over to her and ends their brief conversation with the following statement, "'You sure look pretty in the morning sun," before turning away and mounting his horse. The camera shot then shows him riding away, up a grassy hill above the town, while Cora stands wrapped in a blanket on the porch watching. Just over halfway up the hill, he stops his horse and slowly turns around to look at her. She raises a hand and waves as he stares back at her for a few seconds before turning and riding away.

We have all heard it said, some of us may have even said it to others or had it said to us; boys do not or should not cry. Our culture ingrains this notion in us through the unwritten rules of manhood, something we all have been witness to through entertainment and even in our homes, the belief that boys should not and do not cry, and especially cowboys. At least never let them see you cry, for that is a weakness, especially for men.

Get up, walk it off, rub some dirt on it, you will be okay, and when you have to, just ride away from it. I have lived my life this way, and sometimes, I have had no tears, and when the tears in private do come, they seemed so futile. I am not sure how to live with some of these lies. The world lies, everyone lies, and I am no different, and in those moments, I find myself asking God where the grace is, grace for ourselves and for others.

Warrior Poets

> They are lovers and they are fight-
> ers. They are warrior poets.
> —John Lovell

I am learning that tears are not a weakness; my emotions and feelings make me who I am. I am a warrior poet, fighting for the hearts and souls of others, and to feel makes me stronger in my fight. According to John Lovell, founder of the Warrior Poet Society, it is an ethos. To be the protector we are called to be, we must accept, acknowledge, and nurture both the warrior and poet inside of each man.

While sitting in the present and pondering my future, I can see myself in the past riding Blaze as he continues walking down the dusty road, the solitude, the eternal, and the wisdom of nature surround and invade me. I feel God. I feel his spirit. And the loneliness, if only for brief moments, has receded and faded. I am here, I am alive, and I am strong. The trees do not care if I cry as a soft summer wind whispers through the pine treetops, gently bending the branches back and forth.

I am alone in the wild, a man and a horse, walking forward into a future that leads to where, I do not know, an unknown future and a path that is anything but clear. I am content. The feelings of confusion lay silent for now, and I silently wish I could just ride farther up and until into the sunset, not looking back. For tomorrow is a new day, and I could be in a new place and be anyone I want to be. Riding off from death, I stuff my feelings of pain and loss, for this is my path I have chosen.

The clop of Blaze's hoofs beat rhythmically on the hard-packed dirt road. I am lost in the gentle swaying, my mind a million miles away. I want to ride to unknown lands. I want to search for her, holding a hope that I may find her wherever she is. So forward we go, a young man astraddle a horse on the twenty-ninth year of his birth. My eyes are dry as the sun shines brightly overhead, and I can feel the heat of the day. Long ago, I believed the lie and have carried it as I journeyed through my valley of shadows, boys are not supposed to cry.

Only in the past few years in particular, I am learning that the belief I have chosen is false and can change. I struggle with the past, I carry the shame and regret, constantly asking for forgiveness for sins repeated. I would not have chosen a different path had I known she would die, but now I am choosing a different path moving forward into the future. My grief is a way of loving what was, what is, and what still can be. And maybe, just maybe, I am beginning to believe that it is okay for cowboys and warrior poets to cry.

CONCLUSION

Warrior, Poet, Writer, and a Cowboy

There are things that gnaw at a
man worse than dying.
—Charley Waite, *Open Range*

As we come to the end of this book, another scene from the movie *Open Range* dances in my mind. The two main characters find themselves in a conversation with the townspeople inside the café. Costner's character rebuffs the men there who claim they are not fighters, saying that they are men, aren't they? He further stated that they might not know it, but there are worse things than dying that gnaw at a man. This smacks of truth that my dying does not gnaw at me as much as the death and suffering of those around me that I could not then nor now prevent or stop.

The reality that is to come is that each must venture alone into the alone, and any attempts to thwart that reality are in vain. Looking back, I silently stood and held lightly the very hand that I soon must let go. There was very little crazy or out-there drama all on its own. There was only the forward motion of the hands of eternity that swept her up and took her from this world while I silently cried and broke inside.

Each new day, each new week, each new month, and each New Year, we are granted a second chance. If life is not working the way we had hoped, it is within our power to choose a different path. We do not have a choice with the cards we hold in life, but we owe it to others and ourselves to play the hell out of the hand life deals us.

We all have choices we can make:

- Light or dark
- Night or day
- Sunrise or sunset
- Happy or sad
- Joy or sorrow
- Blessed or dejected
- Love or hate

This is to name a few, and one of the biggest choices we can make is choosing self-compassion, realizing we are imperfect beings living in an imperfect world, and all is usually not as it could be. However, we have hope and are free to choose hope each moment of each day, especially when a connection or relationship goes away, ending in the finality of death, the death of someone young with no one to blame, not your fault, not their fault, nobody's fault. The universe and time just marches on and leaves us to wonder. What do you do with that, especially when the silence ensues?

It is when the house and the rooms of my heart are empty and oh so quiet, almost forsaken, that I finally turn to the one who I believe would understand. They crucified his son, and he could have stopped it but stood by, silently watching, as a sacrifice was made for all humanity.

I look to the heavens, watching sunrises and sunsets, the glory of colors, the majesty as the night turns to day, and the day turns to night. Billowy white clouds sometimes float across the palette of blue in an endless sky uninterrupted by time.

The dark of night and a billion stars twinkle on unconcerned overhead. I have asked the questions I know only he can answer, those questions I long to know, about the mystery and the why behind. I scream, I cajole, I whisper my requests, some with power and fury that frightens even me, others with a tentative prayer. It all seems so simple for the one who spoke the world into existence with a word.

Expectantly, hopefully, I have been waiting all these years, and I have nothing, only silence. I hear no audible word of comfort, understanding, or anything from the one who knows all, simply a whisper, *"Trust me."* However, in the silence, I also see the glory, the majesty, and the power of this thing we call life, the moments, the few years we spend on this physical plane, only a foretaste of that which is to come as we are all journeying into the undiscovered.

My hope sustains me, for there are so many things I have yet to see or hear. Therefore, I dare to hope, and I dare to dream that someday, yes someday, it will all make sense, or better yet, that it will not matter at all.

Full Circle

What once seemed like there was no chance it would ever happen is now a reality. My daughter has owned her own horse for several years now. He is a full-blooded Polish Arabian gelding, Silver Sight, aka Thomas. Who knew this is the way our lives would go?

Death once took all I had and all I ever hoped to have. Yet, God in his mercy has seen fit to grant me so many second chances. The dream of one day again being around horses, getting to ride, and even owning our own has come true through my daughter, our daughter, a child my wife and I for so many years thought was impossible. My life has truly come full circle.

Her love of horses and all animals has given me new opportunities that I thought, with the responsibilities of adulthood and fatherhood, were long gone. The sacrifices of time and money have been so worth it and a whirlwind of activity all around horses.

There have been riding lessons on a borrowed horse and participating in performance shows. Eventually, buying our horse led to more training and competitions, and trail rides into the mountains. The best part is we have seen our daughter happy, motivated, and learning responsibility, and that is PRICELESS!

It was my daughter's dream to have her own horse. It was also my dream, and it took me over fifty years to realize, even if it is vicariously through her. Never stop chasing and believing in the power of your dreams for God can and does often restore what was lost.

I have often stood by my wife's side watching our daughter ride, whether in competitions, in the covered or outdoor arenas, in the fields around the barn, or crossing the street and heading into the mountains for a trail ride. *Who is this smart, strong, passionate, and beautiful young lady that God has graced me with through the unconditional love of a wonderful woman I call my wife*, I wonder as tears of gratitude fill my eyes. And to quote Gandalf in the *Return of the King* by J.R.R. Tolkien, "Go in peace! I will not say: do not weep; for not all tears are an evil."

I am a widower, a husband, a father, a man, a warrior, a writer, a poet, and a cowboy, and I am learning how to cry. I will continue to fight and protect those I love and others in need. I will write poetry and stories of hope that will encourage and strengthen others, speaking of a greater truth, and I will never stop being a cowboy.

> *They say that men are not supposed to cry*
> *Just another bulls—— lie*
> *You will never see tears fall from his eyes*
> *Just another bulls—— lie*
> *And piece by piece is how a man's soul dies*
> *Just another bulls—— lie*

REFERENCES

Clerk, N. W. [pseud.], and C. S. Lewis. 1961. *A Grief Observed*. London, United Kingdom: Faber and Faber Ltd.

Costner, K., dir. 2003. *Open Range*. Motion picture on DVD. United States: Buena Vista Pictures.

Devine, Megan. 2018. *It's Ok That You're Not Ok: Meeting Grief and Loss in a Culture That Doesn't Understand*. Boulder, CO: Sounds True.

Jackson, P., dir. 2001. *The Lord of the Rings: The Fellowship of the Ring*. Motion picture on DVD. New Zealand/United States: New Line Home Entertainment.

Jackson, P., dir. 2004. *The Lord of the Rings: The Return of the King*. Motion picture on DVD. New Zealand/United States/United Kingdom/Germany/China: New Line Cinema.

Jenkinson, Stephen. 2017. *Die Wise: A Manifesto for Sanity and Soul*. Berkley, CA: North Atlantic Book

Lewis, C. S. 1976. *A Grief Observed: A Masterpiece of Rediscovered Faith Which Has Comforted Thousands*. New York, NY: Bantam.

Lewis, C. S. 2009. *In Mere Christianity: A Revised and Amplified Edition, with a New Introduction, of the Three Books Broadcast Talks, Christian Behaviour, and Beyond Personality*. New York, NY: Harper One.

Lewis, C. S. 1949. *The Weight of Glory: and Other Essays*. New York, NY: Macmillan.

Lewis, C. S., and Walter Hooper. 2005. *The Collected Letters of C.S. Lewis*. San Francisco, CA: Harper San Francisco.

Lovell, John. 2017. "Why I Started the Warrior Poet Society." Web log. *Warrior Poet Society* (blog). January 18, 2017. https://warriorpoetsociety.us/why-i-started-the-warrior-poet-society/.

Lovell, John. 2017. "'Beware the Warrior Poet' Poem." Web log. *Warrior Poet Society* (blog), January 17, 2017. https://warriorpoetsociety.us/beware-the-warrior-poet-poem/#more-197.

May, Kate Torgovnick, and Liz Jacobs. 2013. "Death Is Not the End: Fascinating Funeral Traditions from around the Globe." IDEAS.TED.COM. October 1, 2013. https://ideas.ted.com/11-fascinating-funeral-traditions-from-around-the-globe/.

McMurtry, Larry. 1985. *Lonesome Dove, A Novel*. New York, NY: Simon and Schuster.

Mulcahy, R., dir. 1986. *Highlander*. Motion picture on DVD. United Kingdom: Columbia-Cannon-Warner.

Neeld, Elizabeth Harper. 1989. *Seven Choices*. New York, NY: CN Potter.

Scott, R., dir. 2000. *Gladiator*. Motion picture on DVD. United States: Dreamworks L.L.C and Universal Studios.

Seuss, Dr. 1957. *How the Grinch Stole Christmas*. New York, NY: Random House Books.

Sherman, G., dir. 1971. *Big Jake*. Motion picture on DVD. United States: Cinema Center Films through National General Pictures.

Swazey, Kelli. 2013. "Life That Doesn't End with Death." TED. TEDMED., April 2013. https://www.ted.com/talks/kelli_swazey_life_that_doesn_t_end_with_death.

Wincer, S., dir. 1989. *Lonesome Dove*. Motion picture on TV Miniseries. United States: Qintex Entertainment.

Wincer, S., dir. 1990. *Quigley Down Under*. Motion picture on DVD. Australia/United States: Metro-Goldwyn-Mayer.

ABOUT THE AUTHOR

Mark W. Schutter believes we each must be the hero of our own life's story, for no one else could be. He fights for others, seeks truth, writes poetry and stories while often stumbling along the way. He has navigated the pain of loss and grief to find hope and love again. Taking his journal entries and other writings, he has penned his first book, *Cowboys Are Not Supposed to Cry*, a memoir. Grief is not something you just get over, and his book tells his story of living a life while carrying grief. He has poems published in several poetry anthologies on the topics of love, loss, grief, healing, hope, and self-discovery under the pen name Mark Wayne. He has worked in customer service, human resources, organizational development and change management positions, helping others navigate their own life changes. He is currently editing his three-part novel series *The Chronicles of Faith* for publication and he continues to work on other writing projects as well. Mark resides in the Pacific Northwest with his wife and daughter, exploring dusty back roads, always searching for his next great adventure. You can connect with Mark on his website www.markschutter.com.

CPSIA information can be obtained
at www.ICGtesting.com
Printed in the USA
BVHW092314140921
616744BV00012B/601

9 781639 031023